HOW TO KEEP YOUR PLANTS ALIVE

HOW TO KEEP YOUR PLANTS ALIVE

NO GREEN THUMB
50+ PLANTS THAT ARE IMPOSSIBLE TO KILL
NECESSARY

Kit Carlson, PhD, and Aaron Carlson

CIDER MILL PRESS

BOOK PUBLISHERS

CONTENTS

THE HOME AS A PLANT HABITAT

There is a well-known saying in the tree-care industry that simply states, "Put the right tree in the right place," to remind growers that every tree species has unique characteristics and growth requirements that need to be considered before siting it in the landscape. That statement can be applied to all plants and guide you as you think about which plants to bring into your home and where they should be located. Every avid plant enthusiast can relate to the struggle to keep a particular plant species alive. A good example is Rex Begonia *(Begonia rex)*. Some sources claim they are among the easiest houseplants to grow, and others (myself included) find them fussy. Sometimes these challenges can be explained by the fundamental environmental conditions inside the home. Returning to the Rex Begonia example, my house is drafty, with a lot of temperature fluctuations, and, therefore, not ideal for plants like Begonias that have large, delicate leaves.

Before purchasing a plant, you should determine if it is suitable for the conditions you can provide in your home. The light, temperature, and humidity requirements of a particular plant will largely determine whether you can grow it successfully. In other words, can you provide these conditions and maintain them consistently? Consider the available light sources, hours of light, and light intensity in the room you are planning to place your plants in. Be thoughtful about the traffic flow into and out of your home. Doorways that open to the outside create blasts of cold air in the winter, and the resulting drafts can damage sensitive leaves. Do not locate your plants near heating or cooling registers, as they will quickly dry out potting soil. Consider how children or pets might interact with the plants in your home. Will a wagging dog's tail knock the plant over or damage the foliage? Is the plant toxic to pets or humans? All of this should be considered to "put the right plant in the right place." Doing these assessments of your home and how your home is used, as well as becoming familiar with a few characteristics of your plants, can make all the difference in your ability to cultivate and maintain a healthy plant collection.

LIGHT

Some amount of sunlight is required by all photosynthetic plants to survive, grow, and reproduce. Over time, every species has adapted and evolved to thrive in the light conditions that are in its natural environment. Species that grow on the ground in densely forested habitats are adapted to low light levels, as they are constantly in the shade of the other taller species around them. Conversely, plants that occupy habitats with sparse vegetation or that are devoid of taller species, such as in a desert, are adapted to very high levels of light and may be subjected to direct sunlight from sunrise to sunset. Trying to grow a plant in a lighting environment that is drastically different from its natural environment will most likely prove to be fatal to the plant. Some species are more adaptable or resilient than others and may be able to survive in a different lighting environment, but they will likely be less healthy, grow very slowly, fail to flower, and/or be more susceptible to pathogens. Therefore, before selecting a plant for your home or office, you should be keenly aware of the type of light environment it offers and select only plants that thrive in that amount of light.

There are three general categories of intensity that can be used to describe the light environment inside, as well as the preference of a particular species. They are bright light, medium light, and low light. These categories are defined by the light intensity, measured in lumens or lux (historically, foot-candles), at a particular location. Inexpensive light meters can be purchased that will measure light intensity and can assist you in choosing the right plants for your home or office.

Lighting can further be characterized by how the light is delivered to a particular location. Direct light is light that hits an area in a straight line, directly from the sun, unimpeded and unaltered by any type of object other than glass. Indirect light is light that has been altered in some way prior to hitting a particular location. Examples of things that can impede light are other plants (indoor or outdoor), exterior buildings, curtains, and/or furniture. Light reflected off a surface can also be considered indirect light. The type and intensity of light will change throughout the year as the trajectory of the sun changes in the sky. This could impact the light environment indoors enough that it transitions from one category to another over the course of a year. Artificial lights are often used to counter seasonal light changes or to increase the lumens present in a particular location.

BRIGHT LIGHT ranges from 1,614 to 10,764 lux. Indoors, bright light only occurs near south- or west-facing windows that receive direct sunlight for at least six hours a day. It should be noted that many plants adapted to bright light may suffer from cold drafts that can come from the window during colder times of the year. These plants should be moved farther away from the window during those periods, and artificial lights may be needed to maintain a bright light environment.

MEDIUM LIGHT ranges from 807 to 1,614 lux. A medium light environment is one that receives only indirect light or direct light for a short time each day. Indoors, a medium light environment can typically be found near east-facing windows or south- or west-facing windows that have trees nearby or are covered by curtains that allow some light through. You can also achieve medium light in a room with a south- or west-facing window by positioning the plant farther away from the window.

LOW LIGHT ranges from 270 to 807 lux. Most indoor locations in your home or office probably fall into this category. North-facing windows usually produce low light environments, as do windows in which the blinds are kept shut most of the time. Any location that is at least 2.5 meters from a window will also fall into this category. Artificial light by itself usually produces only a low light environment as well. A good rule of thumb is that if it is difficult to read a newspaper, you are probably in a low light environment.

Besides augmenting window light with artificial light, there are other things that you can do to increase the light environment for your plant(s). For example, you can use mirrors to reflect sunlight onto the plant, move the plant closer to a window, and dust off the plant's leaves periodically. To decrease light levels, you can create shade by incorporating taller plants, reduce the amount of reflected light by painting walls a dark color, or move the plant farther away from natural light sources.

TEMPERATURE AND HUMIDITY

Just as plants have adapted to thrive in their native light environment, they are also adapted to the climate of their native habitat, which is primarily influenced by geography. Where a plant naturally grows determines the range and seasonality of the temperatures and humidity levels it has adapted to and evolved in. To successfully grow a particular plant indoors, you must be mindful of its temperature and humidity requirements. Plants from arid environments will not cope well in a space with high humidity. Tropical plants do not like cold temperatures. Fortunately, many houseplants do well in the temperatures and humidity levels common in most homes. However, the temperature and humidity in any given house will vary spatially and seasonally. A house's south- and west-facing rooms are likely to be warmer than the north- and east-facing rooms, especially when the sun is shining. During the winter, there can be a cold microclimate close to a window that may affect many plants. Also, the drafts created by heating and cooling systems can cause sudden, and drastic, temperature changes that plants are not naturally subjected to, and they may suffer if placed too close to a vent. Furthermore, these drafts can cause the soil to dry out more quickly.

If a plant is too warm or cold or too wet or dry, its overall health will suffer, and it may not survive. These factors all need to be considered when choosing the type of houseplant and its placement in your home or office.

The temperature requirements of plants can be divided into three main categories: warm, cool, and cold. Warm generally refers to temperatures above 20°C/68°F, cool ranges from 15°C/59°F to 20°C/68°F, and cold is below 15°C/59°F. Plants that prefer warm temperatures usually come from tropical parts of the world, at low to mid elevations. These plants are adapted to experiencing the same temperature year-round. They may not survive even brief exposure to cold temperatures. Plants that prefer cool temperatures are usually from subtropical areas of the world or high elevations in tropical regions. These plants are adapted to some seasonal temperature differences, although freezing temperatures are, at most, an infrequent occurrence. Plants that prefer cold temperatures can come from locations all over the world, from areas that never get very warm or are warm for only a short time of the year. They may or may not be frost hardy.

As with temperature, the average humidity of any particular location is primarily a function of its geography, which significantly influences the amount of moisture in the air at any given time and place. Plants have evolved and adapted to the humidity regime of their natural environment. The humidity requirements of plants can also be divided into three categories, based on the percent concentration of water vapor in the air: high humidity is generally above 60%, moderate humidity ranges from 40% to 60%, and low humidity is below 40%. Most modern homes with heating and cooling systems maintain low humidity levels. This creates an indoor environment that is not humid enough for many houseplants, except those from arid habitats. Therefore, houseplants native to humid climates require implementing strategies to increase the humidity where they are growing. One way to achieve this is to grow several (or more) plants relatively close together. Water that evaporates from the soil and transpires from the plants creates a humid microclimate in their immediate vicinity. Another strategy is to place a saucer full of pebbles and water under the plant's container. Similarly, placing the plant's container inside a larger container and filling the space between them with damp sphagnum moss will increase the humidity. Using a humidifier is another option, as well as putting plants in a naturally humid area, such as a kitchen or bathroom.

GROWING CONTAINER

The container your plant grows in can be just as important as the proper temperature, humidity, and soil, and it can significantly influence the overall health of the plant. Containers come in a vast array of sizes and shapes and are made from a variety of different materials. All of these factors will affect the plant and need to be considered when making your selection.

SIZE: A container that is too big may remain too wet for too long after watering, which could suffocate the plant or lead to health problems such as root rot. A container that is too small will quickly cause the plant to become root-bound. This is because, as the plant's roots grow and expand, they are constrained by the walls of the container, causing them to grow in circles, girdling themselves in the process. At the same time, the roots break down the soil particles and absorb their nutrients. Eventually, you end up with a container filled with mostly roots and an insufficient amount of soil, which negatively impacts the plant's health. As a general rule, the diameter or width of a container should be approximately one-third the height of the plant, and you should plan on repotting the plant into a larger container every couple of years.

SHAPE: The shape of a container should be matched to the type of root system the plant has. Plants with shallow root systems, such as cacti, should be planted in shallow containers. Plants that produce a taproot, such as *Lithops*, should be planted in containers sufficiently deep so that the downward growth of the taproot does not reach the bottom of the pot.

MATERIAL: Most plant containers are made of plastic or clay. They both have their advantages and disadvantages. Plastic pots are more inexpensive and durable than clay pots; however, they retain water longer than clay pots and are more prone to overwatering. In unglazed clay pots, moisture is able to evaporate through the sides of the container, which promotes soil aeration and overall plant health, but the soil dries out faster and requires more frequent waterings than in a plastic container.

Perhaps the most important thing to look for when choosing a container is to make sure it has at least one drainage hole. Drainage holes allow excess salts to leach out and keep the soil in the lower part of the container aerated. Without drainage holes, water will accumulate at the bottom, eventually becoming anoxic, which can promote the growth of microbes that can be detrimental to the plant, not to mention produce a disagreeable odor.

GROWING MEDIUM

When a plant is grown in a container, it will need something a bit different from the soil it is naturally found in. This is because the plant is limited to the medium within the container to provide the conditions and nutrients needed to grow and thrive. There are a wide variety of potting mixes on the market today, from generic "potting soil" to mixes that are formulated for specific types of plants. Many commercial mixes are soilless and made primarily from peat. Generally speaking, a good growing medium should include coarse particles like sand or perlite to help keep the soil aerated, as well as organic matter, such as peat moss, to hold water and prevent the soil from becoming compacted. It should also contain a source of nutrients that the plant can readily uptake through its roots, such as a slow-release fertilizer or compost. Regardless of the mix you use, over time its volume in the pot will decrease from settling and from the plant breaking down organic matter. When this occurs, the soil will become less aerated and start retaining more water. Repotting or mixing in fresh soil periodically should help prevent this from happening.

There are a variety of mixes that are formulated specifically for certain types of plants. For example, a growing medium composed almost entirely of bark works very well for epiphytes. For plants that grow in sandy, arid regions, such as cacti, a mix composed largely of sand can be used. These plants are not adapted to moisture-retaining substrates and can quickly rot if not grown in a well-drained medium. Succulents typically thrive best in a substrate of about 50% sand and/or perlite and 50% potting soil.

It is often less expensive to purchase individual components and mix your own rather than buy a premade mix. Some staples to keep on hand in tubs include peat, bark, perlite, vermiculite, gravel, coir, and potting soil.

An alternative to traditional potting mixes is the use of hydroponics. In simple terms, hydroponics means growing plants without soil. Instead, the plants are grown in water with specially designed nutrients added to it that provide the plants with everything they need to thrive, as well as something to maintain an ideal pH, if needed. A hydroponic system can be as simple as a jar of water, which acts as both the container and soil, or it can be a high-tech system with several components, such as pumps and aerators that manipulate the water. The latter is usually used in commercial operations, because the size, cost, and maintenance is too much for most people to handle on their own. For the most part, plants raised hydroponically will grow bigger and faster than those grown in potting soil. The primary disadvantage to using a hydroponic system is the need to monitor the water much more closely to ensure that the nutrient concentration and pH are within the desired range. Some examples of plants that particularly benefit from a hydroponic system are *Monstera*, *Philodendron*, and *Pothos*.

WATER

The most crucial part of caring for a houseplant is watering. Common houseplant problems can often be traced back to overwatering or underwatering. It is essential to understand the water requirements of your houseplants and their growing conditions (soil, container, light, humidity, etc.), so that you know how often to water them and how much water to apply when you do.

The watering method should also be considered. Excessive water on leaf surfaces can leave brown spots and necrosis in some plants, including African Violets and Bird's-Nest Ferns. Applying water from the bottom up, sometimes referred to as bottom watering, can be a useful strategy to prevent overwatering and avoid exposing sensitive leaves to water. In bottom watering, a potted plant is placed into a shallow container of water, using just enough water to cover the bottom few centimeters of the pot. After 20–30 minutes, the upper soil surface should feel moistened, and the plant can be removed from the water.

You should also be familiar with the quality of the water you use on your plants. Some plants, like *Nepenthes* and *Sarracenia*, are very sensitive to salts and metals, and distilled water should be used. You should avoid using softened water on almost all houseplants. If you have a water softener, use water that does not go through your system.

FERTILIZER

When a plant is grown in a container, there is a finite amount of nutrients in the soil. When this supply is exhausted, the plant's overall health will deteriorate. Therefore, it is essential to periodically replenish the supply with fertilizer. A wide variety of fertilizers are available, not only in their nutrient concentrations but also in how they are delivered. The plant's cultural requirements need to be considered when selecting the type of fertilizer to use. Most fertilizers contain nitrogen, phosphorus, and potassium as the primary components, in various concentrations that are usually displayed as a percentage of concentration on the packaging. For example, a 5-10-10 fertilizer is 5% nitrogen, 10% phosphorus, and 10% potassium. Most plants will grow well with a fertilizer that has equal (or close to it) concentrations of nitrogen, phosphorus, and potassium.

Most fertilizers are sold in one of two forms. There is soluble fertilizer that is usually sold as a dry powder, dissolved in water and applied to the growth medium, or slow-release fertilizer, consisting of pellets that are deposited directly on the surface of the growth medium, and that release a small quantity of nutrients every time the plant is watered. For many houseplants, slow-release fertilizers are more efficient and user-friendly, with limited risk of causing nitrogen burns on leaves from overfertilizing. Regardless of the type of fertilizer you use, it is important to carefully follow the manufacturer's instructions. Too much fertilizer can be lethal to plants, and different kinds of plants have unique needs. For example, most cacti do not require much fertilizer. A general rule of thumb for cacti is to fertilize them with a standard liquid fertilizer that is diluted by at least half the manufacturer's instructions. Ferns are similarly sensitive to fertilizer; an application of a slow-release fertilizer several times a year during the spring and summer is a good standard of practice for most ferns.

PROPAGATION AND GERMINATION TECHNIQUES

Every plant species will have unique considerations for plant propagation and seed germination. Many plants can be propagated by stem cuttings. A successful stem cutting will result in a genetically identical daughter plant. The specific strategy used will vary by species, but a typical best practice would involve excising a freshly growing stem section 5 cm to 10 cm long. The stem cutting should have leaves or leaf nodes. The lower leaves on the cutting should be carefully removed. The end of the stem can be dipped in a rooting hormone and placed in water or potted in soil. Once planted, the cutting needs to be kept moist and placed in a location with bright but indirect light. Over time, roots will begin to develop from the bottom of the cutting, and new growth will emerge from the top. Eventually, the cutting will form a new plant that is genetically identical to the parent plant.

Many common fern species can be propagated using rhizome cuttings. Rhizomes are underground stems that grow more horizontally than aboveground stems. To make a rhizome cutting, the rhizome should be carefully dug up, and a short 5 cm to 10 cm section should be excised. The excised rhizome should be buried horizontally and kept moist. Ferns can also be started from the spores that form on the undersides of the fern fronds. These spores are contained in structures called sori. To propagate a fern from spores, collect the spores by placing a frond with mature spores into a paper bag and gently shaking.

Sprinkle the spores onto a pot filled with a mixture of peat moss and sand or perlite. Keep the pot moist and covered with plastic to maintain humidity until the spores germinate and develop into young fern gametophytes. These will eventually produce gametes that result in zygote formation and a new mature fern.

Seed germination from houseplant seeds can be quite challenging. Very frequently, flowers and seeds do not form on houseplants grown indoors, due to a lack of light and other conditions required for flowering and seed set. When seeds are available, germination techniques will vary based on the plant species. A tropical species is more likely to produce seeds that are ready to germinate soon after fruit maturity. A species that is native to a climate with a long, cold winter typically requires a cold-stratificaiton period before germination will occur.

PLANT PROFILES

USING THIS BOOK

This book will introduce you to dozens of houseplants selected for their beauty, variety, and culture requirements that make them easy to maintain and adaptable to a range of conditions. For each plant, the scientific and common names are listed, followed by a botanical description of its basic identifying characteristics, its region of origin, and the type of habitat it naturally grows in. This is followed by cultivation and care information that lists the plant's light, temperature, humidity, growing media, watering and fertilizer requirements, and information about its flowering and propagation. We also provide recommendations for pet-safe (nontoxic) plants. At the back of the book, you can find a glossary of helpful terms and a table with a matrix of soil moisture and lighting conditions for every plant found in these pages.

NOTE: None of these species are intended to be ingested, and information pertaining to pet and human safety should be considered only a recommendation. Always refer to a veterinarian or medical doctor should you have any concerns about ingestion or exposure to poisonous plants.

LIPSTICK PLANT SEE PAGE 32

CHINESE EVERGREEN SEE PAGE 34

SCIENTIFIC NAME: *Aeschynanthus radicans*
COMMON NAME: Lipstick Plant
FAMILY: Gesneriaceae

DESCRIPTION: An epiphytic (growing on other plants) vine that grows up to 1.5 m long, usually hanging from, or sprawling along, tree branches. The leaves are found in opposite pairs, lanceolate in shape with an entire margin, and up to 8 cm long. They are dark green and fleshy and usually very numerous along the stem. The inflorescence is a terminal cluster of bright-red tubular flowers, with some rarer varieties having yellow or orange flowers.

DISTRIBUTION: It naturally occurs in Malaysian rain forests.

CULTIVATION AND CARE

LIGHT: Bright to medium indirect
TEMPERATURE: Warm
HUMIDITY: High

GROWING MEDIA: It will thrive in various soil mixes but performs best in a light, well-aerated, well-drained mix. Soil mixes designed for African Violets are also appropriate.

WATERING: The soil should be kept moist during the active growth period of spring and summer. Allow the top inch/ several centimeters of the soil surface to dry before watering again. Pots should have good drainage. Bottom watering is best.

During the dormant winter period, water less frequently.

FERTILIZER: Fertilize the plant every four to six weeks with a slow-release indoor plant fertilizer during the active growth period. Do not fertilize during the dormant season.

FLOWERING: In the proper growing environment, the Lipstick Plant will flower indoors throughout the growing season. Bright, indirect light promotes flowering.

PROPAGATION: New plants can be started from stem cuttings.

DID YOU KNOW...

- Indoors, the vining habit of the Lipstick Plant makes it a good option for hanging baskets.
- The genus name (*Aeschynanthus*) means "red shame," while the species name (*radicans*) means "rooting stems."
- *Aeschynanthus* is nontoxic to pets and humans.

SCIENTIFIC NAME: *Aglaonema* spp.
COMMON NAME: Chinese Evergreen
FAMILY: Araceae

DESCRIPTION: A genus of evergreen perennials that can be erect, or low-growing, sprawling plants, depending on the species. They are generally under 1.5 m in height or length and feature elliptical or lanceolate dark-green leaves around 20 cm long that are variegated to some degree. Numerous hybrids and cultivars have been developed, each with a unique combination of colors and variegation patterns. The flower is a white spadix partially surrounded by a pale-green spathe. They tend to remain hidden under the leaves and are rarely produced in cultivation.

DISTRIBUTION: It is native to tropical forests of Southeast Asia and New Guinea.

CULTIVATION AND CARE

LIGHT: Medium to low. Bright light should be avoided.

TEMPERATURE: Warm

HUMIDITY: High

GROWING MEDIA: Use a light, well-aerated, well-draining mix.

WATERING: The soil should be kept moist during the active growth period of spring and summer. Allow the top inch/

several centimeters of the soil to dry before watering again. Pots should have good drainage. Bottom watering is best. During the dormant winter period, water less frequently. Be careful not to overwater.

FERTILIZER: These plants do not require a lot of fertilizer. One application of diluted indoor houseplant fertilizer in the spring is sufficient.

FLOWERING: This plant is primarily grown for its beautiful foliage but will flower under the right conditions. Adequate lighting is the most critical factor influencing flowering, with blooming most likely to occur in late winter or early spring.

PROPAGATION: *Aglaonema* species tend to be slow growing in cultivation and even prefer growing in a slightly root-bound condition. Every two to three years, plants can be repotted and divided. Ensure each division includes roots and basal shoots. Propagation from stem cuttings is also possible, but stems should have multiple leaves and nodes, appearing as small white dots along the stems.

DID YOU KNOW...

- Some *Aglaonema* growers remove flower buds to ensure the energy expenditure of flowering does not reduce leaf size and beauty.
- *Aglaonema* is toxic to pets and humans.

ALOCASIA, ELEPHANT'S EAR SEE PAGE 38

ALOE SEE PAGE 40

SCIENTIFIC NAME: *Alocasia* spp.
COMMON NAME: Alocasia, Elephant's Ear
FAMILY: Araceae

DESCRIPTION: A genus of tuberous herbaceous perennials (around 90 species), appearing as clumps of long-stalked leaves that grow from stems that emerge from the underground rhizome. Plants can reach heights of up to 4 m. The leaves are sagittate to cordate in shape, can reach lengths of up to 90 cm, and feature prominent leaf veins that create a textured appearance. In many varieties, these veins are colored white, creating a striking contrast to the dark-green leaf tissue. In other varieties, the leaf margins may be crinkled or ruffled and feature a variety of colorations and patterns. The flowers are typical spathe/spadix flowers seen in the Arum family and are usually hidden by the leaves.

DISTRIBUTION: It is native to tropical rain forests of Southeast Asia and Australia.

CULTIVATION AND CARE

LIGHT: Bright indirect

TEMPERATURE: Warm

HUMIDITY: High

GROWING MEDIA: It thrives best in most commercially available soil mixes. Adding amendments such as perlite, orchid bark mix, or coconut coir to a standard mix can improve drainage and aeration.

WATERING: During the active growth period of spring and summer, it should be watered thoroughly and allowed to dry out slightly between waterings, although some varieties can be kept moist. Watering should be reduced in the dormant winter months.

FERTILIZER: Fertilize bimonthly with a balanced indoor plant fertilizer during the active growth period. It does not require fertilizer during the dormant months.

FLOWERING: Mature plants may produce flowers during summer, but they are prized for their beautiful foliage, and some growers will remove flowers to promote foliage growth.

PROPAGATION: Stem and leaf cuttings do not work to propagate *Alocasia* spp. New growth arises from underground stems or corms. After several years of development, mature plants can be divided, and the corms or tubers can be split into new pots.

DID YOU KNOW...

- Some commercially available *Alocasia* plants are propagated from tissue culture and may not have the energy reserves to form a corm during their first growing season.
- Some species have been cultivated for over 20,000 years, using the corms as a food source.
- Many believe that the plant in *Jack and the Beanstalk* is based on *Alocasia*.
- *Alocasia* is mildly toxic to pets and humans.

SCIENTIFIC NAME: *Aloe vera*
COMMON NAME: Aloe
FAMILY: Asphodelaceae

DESCRIPTION: A stemless evergreen perennial succulent with rosettes of thick, stiff, upright leaves reaching up to 1 m in height. The fleshy leaves are grayish green and often spotted with tiny white dots. The margins are serrated, with small white teeth. The gel-like sap in the leaves has long been used as a topical treatment for minor skin injuries, such as burns, dry skin, and wounds. The yellow flowers are borne in erect racemes that extend above the tips of the leaves and are only produced in cultivation under optimal growing conditions.

DISTRIBUTION: It is native to tropical arid habitats of the Arabian Peninsula and North Africa, but is widely established in similar habitats around the world.

CULTIVATION AND CARE

LIGHT: Bright indirect

TEMPERATURE: Warm to cool

HUMIDITY: Low to moderate

GROWING MEDIA: Performs best in a light, well-aerated, well-draining mix.

WATERING: Water moderately during the spring and summer, allowing the pot to dry out between waterings. Reduce watering during the late fall and winter.

FERTILIZER: These plants do not require a lot of fertilizer. One application of diluted indoor houseplant fertilizer in the spring is sufficient.

FLOWERING: In mature plants, flowering may occur once a year, from late winter to summer. Flowers are showy and may persist for several weeks or even months.

PROPAGATION: Stem cuttings are not an effective propagation strategy for this plant. *Aloe vera* can be propagated by dividing daughter plants into separate pots during repotting. New plants, called "pups," will appear alongside mature growth. These can be transferred to a well-drained growth medium to promote root growth and establishment.

DID YOU KNOW...

- The global *Aloe* industry is predicted to exceed $3 billion by 2030.
- Despite its use as a topical skin treatment, it is potentially toxic if ingested (for both humans and pets).

PAINTER'S PALETTE, FLAMINGO FLOWER, RED ANTHURIUM SEE PAGE 44

NORFOLK ISLAND PINE SEE PAGE 46

SCIENTIFIC NAME: *Anthurium andraeanum*

COMMON NAME: Painter's Palette, Flamingo Flower, Red Anthurium

FAMILY: Araceae

DESCRIPTION: An epiphytic, evergreen perennial. It forms clumps of dark-green heart-shaped leaves up to 20 cm long on stems up to 30 cm long. Solitary flowers emerge between the leaves on similarly sized stalks. The flower consists of a yellowish-colored spadix partially surrounded by a bright, glossy, heart-shaped red spathe up to 15 cm long. Under favorable conditions, the plant will send up long-lasting flowers year-round.

DISTRIBUTION: It is native to the rain forests of northwestern South America.

CULTIVATION AND CARE

LIGHT: Bright indirect

TEMPERATURE: Warm

HUMIDITY: High

GROWING MEDIA: It performs best in a light, well-aerated, well-draining mix. Amending standard potting soil with perlite, bark, or coir is beneficial. Soil mixes designed for African Violets are also appropriate.

WATERING: The soil should be kept moist during the active growth period of spring and summer. Allow the top inch/ several centimeters of the soil to dry before watering again. Pots should have good drainage. Bottom watering is best. During the dormant winter period, water less frequently.

FERTILIZER: Fertilize the plant every three weeks with a slow-release indoor plant fertilizer during the active growth period.

FLOWERING: *Anthurium andraeanum* is grown for its long-lasting, showy flowers. Flowering is more likely to occur when plants receive bright, indirect light and are maintained in a warm (18°C/65°F and up), humid environment.

PROPAGATION: New plants can be started from stem cuttings.

DID YOU KNOW...

· *Anthurium* symbolizes hospitality and makes an excellent housewarming gift.
· *Anthurium* is toxic to pets and humans.

SCIENTIFIC NAME: *Araucaria heterophylla*
COMMON NAME: Norfolk Island Pine
FAMILY: Araucariaceae

DESCRIPTION: A coniferous evergreen tree featuring whorls of four to seven (most commonly five) branches that point straight outward from the trunk. Juvenile leaves are awl-shaped and needlelike, and up to 1.5 cm long. Adult leaves are overlapping, flattened, and scalelike. The bark ranges from gray to brown, with exfoliating scales developing over time. Male cones are held in elongated clusters up to 4 cm long, reddish brown, and with a cylindrical shape. Female cones are globular with a diameter of up to 15 cm, bearing numerous pointed scales. They can get up to 70 m tall in the wild, with trunks nearly 2 m in width. In cultivation, specimens rarely exceed 3 m in height.

DISTRIBUTION: It is native to Norfolk Island, approximately 1,500 km east of Australia. It can be found growing on sea cliffs and inland rain forests.

CULTIVATION AND CARE

LIGHT: Bright indirect

TEMPERATURE: Warm

HUMIDITY: High

GROWING MEDIA: Performs best in a light, well-aerated, well-draining mix.

WATERING: The soil should be kept moist during the active growth period of spring and summer. Pots should have good drainage. During the dormant winter period, water less frequently.

FERTILIZER: Every two weeks, apply a balanced fertilizer for indoor plants during the active growth period. It does not require fertilizer during the dormant months.

FLOWERING: This genus does not produce flowers.

PROPAGATION: In theory, you can propagate a new Norfolk Island Pine by taking stem cuttings, but stem cuttings taken from side branches will always grow like horizontal branches and never grow like a symmetrical tree. A cutting can be made from the top of the tree, but removing this top stem will alter the symmetry and shape of the original plant. A cutting from the top might be recommended if the original plant is no longer attractive and a new start is desired.

DID YOU KNOW...

- *Araucaria heterophylla* was first reported in Western scientific literature by Captain Cook in 1774 and introduced into cultivation in 1793.
- Wild populations have drastically declined due to habitat loss and degradation.
- *Araucaria heterophylla* is potentially toxic to pets.

ASPARAGUS FERN SEE PAGE 50

CAST IRON PLANT SEE PAGE 52

SCIENTIFIC NAME: *Asparagus setaceus*
COMMON NAME: Asparagus Fern
FAMILY: Asparagaceae

DESCRIPTION: A bushy evergreen vine featuring feathery, fernlike cladodes on wiry, spiny stems up to 6 m long. The leaflike cladodes are flattened, modified stems that bear the plant's flowers. The plant's true leaves are small and scalelike. The flowers are greenish white, bell-shaped, and only around 4 mm long.

DISTRIBUTION: It is native to coastal areas of South Africa, where it can be found in sandy and somewhat shady habitats.

CULTIVATION AND CARE

LIGHT: Bright to medium indirect

TEMPERATURE: Warm to cool

HUMIDITY: High

GROWING MEDIA: Performs best in a light, well-aerated, well-draining mix.

WATERING: The soil should be kept moist during the active growth period of spring and summer. Pots should have good drainage. During the dormant winter period, water less frequently.

FERTILIZER: Use a balanced liquid fertilizer every two weeks during the active growth period. It does not require fertilizer during the dormant period.

FLOWERING: Small, fragrant flowers will appear on mature specimens, typically in the early fall. Flowering can be encouraged by maintaining plants in medium to high humidity.

PROPAGATION: Dividing the plant during repotting is the most efficient way to propagate new plants. Seed germination can be challenging, requiring up to a month for seeds to sprout.

DID YOU KNOW...

· Despite its name, the Asparagus Fern is not a true fern and is more closely related to garlic and onions than to ferns!
· Asparagus Ferns are nontoxic to pets and humans.

SCIENTIFIC NAME: *Aspidistra elatior*
COMMON NAME: Cast Iron Plant
FAMILY: Asparagaceae

DESCRIPTION: An herbaceous perennial featuring long-stalked leaves emerging directly from a fleshy rootstock, reaching heights of up to 1 m. Leaves are up to 60 cm long and 10 cm wide, lanceolate in shape, and colored dark, glossy green. Some cultivated varieties bear various white markings (variegation) on the leaves, such as stripes and speckles. Flowers are rarely produced on cultivated plants. They barely emerge from the surface and are fleshy eight-lobed flowers with dark-red coloration.

DISTRIBUTION: It is native to southern Japan, where it is an understory plant in primarily higher-elevation forests.

CULTIVATION AND CARE

LIGHT: Medium to low

TEMPERATURE: Warm to cool

HUMIDITY: Moderate to high

GROWING MEDIA: Any well-draining growth medium is adequate for this plant.

WATERING: It performs best with low to moderate watering. Water adequately and wait for the soil to dry before the next watering.

FERTILIZER: Applying a slow-release fertilizer once or twice during the spring and summer is sufficient.

FLOWERING: This species does not frequently flower in cultivation. When it does bloom, the unique flowers are found at the soil level.

PROPAGATION: The easiest way to propagate *Aspidistra* is to divide daughter plants into separate pots during repotting.

DID YOU KNOW...

· The flowers of *Aspidistra elatior* are believed to be mushroom mimics, attracting fungus gnats that act as pollinators.
· *Aspidistra elatior* is nontoxic to pets and humans.

BIRD'S-NEST FERN SEE PAGE 56

PONYTAIL PALM, ELEPHANT'S FOOT SEE PAGE 58

SCIENTIFIC NAME: *Asplenium nidus*
COMMON NAME: Bird's-Nest Fern
FAMILY: Aspleniaceae

DESCRIPTION: An evergreen epiphytic fern that can reach heights of up to 2 m in the wild, but usually less than 1 m in cultivation. It forms rosettes of upright, arching fronds that result in an overall vaselike appearance. Individual fronds are strap shaped and up to 1 m long and 60 cm wide. They are a bright, glossy light green in color with entire margins that are usually undulating to some extent. The midrib is prominently dark brown to black in color. Spore-producing structures (sori) are produced on the lower surface of the fronds. They are linear in shape, blackish in color, and arranged in a herringbone pattern along the midrib. As individual fronds die, they turn brown and curl up, which over time results in the formation of a bird nest–like structure at the base of the plant.

DISTRIBUTION: They are native to tropical rain forest habitats from Hawaii to Polynesia to Southeast Asia and East Africa, where they are mostly found growing epiphytically on trees, such as palms.

CULTIVATION AND CARE

LIGHT: Bright to low indirect
TEMPERATURE: Warm to cool
HUMIDITY: Moderate to high

GROWING MEDIA: A commercial soil mix designed for ferns or well-drained soil will be appropriate.

WATERING: Plants should be kept moist but not kept in standing water. Avoid getting water on the foliage, as brown spots may appear on the leaves.

FERTILIZER: Ferns can be very sensitive to commercial fertilizers. A dilute (quarter-strength) all-purpose indoor plant fertilizer can be used once or twice during the spring and summer.

FLOWERING: Ferns do not produce flowers.

PROPAGATION: Ferns do not produce seeds, but they do produce spores contained in sori found along the undersurfaces of the leaves. The spores can be germinated using the techniques described earlier in this book (pages 26–27).

DID YOU KNOW...

- This group of ferns belongs to the Spleenwort family and was once believed to be a treatment for diseases of the spleen.
- Many plants sold as *Asplenium nidus* are *Asplenium australasicum*, which is very similar in appearance.
- *Asplenium nidus* is nontoxic to pets and humans.

SCIENTIFIC NAME: *Beaucarnea recurvata*
COMMON NAME: Ponytail Palm, Elephant's Foot
FAMILY: Asparagaceae

DESCRIPTION: A small evergreen tree, up to 10 m in height. It has a single trunk with a prominent enlarged, flaring base. Mature trees eventually start branching at the top of the trunk. At the tips of branches and the main trunk are rosettes of long strap-like leaves, up to 2 m long and 3 cm wide, although they are typically much shorter on cultivated plants. Mature trees will produce long panicles of numerous small greenish-white flowers.

DISTRIBUTION: It is native to desertlike habitats in southeastern Mexico.

CULTIVATION AND CARE

LIGHT: Bright indirect (two to three hours of direct sunlight per day is acceptable)

TEMPERATURE: Cool to warm

HUMIDITY: Low to moderate

GROWING MEDIA: Any standard commercial potting soil will be adequate. Amending a standard potting soil with sand and perlite will improve drainage.

WATERING: Water sparingly and allow the soil to dry between waterings.

FERTILIZER: The Ponytail Palm does not require much fertilizer. An annual application of an all-purpose, slow-release pellet fertilizer in the spring is sufficient.

FLOWERING: Although the Ponytail Palm produces flowers, it rarely blooms when cultivated indoors.

PROPAGATION: New offshoots form along the flared base of the trunk. These "pups" can be carefully extracted and potted to produce new plants.

DID YOU KNOW...

- The swollen trunk of the Ponytail Palm acts as a water storage mechanism.
- Ponytail Palms are nontoxic to pets and humans.

BEGONIA SEE PAGE 62

CALATHEA, ZEBRA PLANT, PRAYER PLANT SEE PAGE 66

SCIENTIFIC NAME: *Begonia* spp.
COMMON NAME: Begonia
FAMILY: Begoniaceae

DESCRIPTION: One of the largest genera of flowering plants, it is composed of over 2,000 species exhibiting a variety of growth forms (annuals, perennials, vines, shrubs, etc.). Their popularity as houseplants, and the vast number of species, has resulted in *Begonia* species being informally divided into seven major groups. These are not taxonomically derived but rather horticulturally. They are:

REX CULTORUM: A large number (more than 4,000) of cultivars that are descendants of an Indian species, *Begonia rex*, that has been hybridized with at least 30 other species. They are rhizomatous Begonias with strikingly colored leaves in various shades of silver, red, purple, and green. The leaves range from simple/entire to bizarre/asymmetrical.

CANE-LIKE: Tall, erect plants with swollen nodes on the stem, superficially resembling bamboo. The leaves are often spotted or have a textural appearance. Flowers are produced nearly year-round in long, cascading clusters. Over 2,000 cultivars are included in this group, descended from at least 80 different species.

RHIZOMATOUS: Begonias in this group have a modified stem (rhizome) used to store water and nutrients. The leaves emerge from the rhizome and tend to form an overall globular-shaped plant. The leaves are quite variable in shape and appearance.

They can be round, kidney-shaped, maple-like, star shaped, or asymmetrical, often with various blotches or spots, depending on the cultivar. Flowers are usually white to pink and are produced primarily in late winter to spring.

SHRUB-LIKE: As the name suggests, these Begonias are multistemmed shrubs, with some species and cultivars reaching nearly 4 m in height. They can be confused with varieties in the cane-like group, but they lack the swollen nodes on their stems and tend to be less floriferous. Leaves are variable, running nearly the gamut of leaf types among the Begonias.

SEMPERFLORENS: These are Wax Begonias, often sold as bedding plants or in hanging baskets, making this group probably the most grown Begonia worldwide. The leaves are thick, waxy, and roundish to cordate in shape, often with a toothed margin, and they range in color from greenish to bronze. Some varieties exhibit leaf variegation. They tend to be nonstop bloomers, with flowers ranging anywhere from white to red. Many cultivars in this group have double flowers.

TUBEROUS: Begonias in this group produce underground tubers, usually at the end of the growing season when the plant goes dormant. This group also boasts the largest and most colorful flowers, although some tuberous Begonias produce small flowers. The bright, large-flowered cultivars are descended from high-altitude species, thus preferring cooler climates than most other types. Other tuberous Begonias include small, bedding plant–like forms with smaller but numerous flowers, and spreading/creeping cultivars that feature hanging or pendulous stems and flowers grown in a pot or hanging basket.

TRAILING/SCANDENT: This group contains creeping or climbing varieties, primarily used in hanging baskets or on trellises. Unlike the other groups, cultivars in this group are primarily pure species and not the result of hybridization, although more and more hybrids are being created in this group. Many cultivars are in bloom all year, and most feature white or pink flowers.

THICK STEMMED: This group may be the most variable, primarily because the only common feature is that they all have prominently thicker stems than the other groups, which become exposed over time as the lower leaves fall off. Otherwise, leaf size, shape, and color runs the full range of all Begonia types.

HIEMALIS, RIEGER, ELATIOR, AND X CHEIMANTHA: This is a large, diverse group of complex hybrids initially derived from the species *Begonia socotrana*, which, unlike most Begonias, flowers during the winter. This was considered a novelty among early Begonia lovers, leading to an ever-increasing number of hybrids being developed.

DISTRIBUTION: They can be found naturally in subtropical and tropical areas of Central and South America, Africa, and Asia.

CULTIVATION AND CARE

LIGHT: Bright indirect

TEMPERATURE: Cool to warm

HUMIDITY: Moderate to high

GROWING MEDIA: Any well-draining potting mix will be adequate for most Begonias.

WATERING: Plants should be watered moderately during the spring and summer, and allowed to become slightly dry between waterings. In the dormant winter period, watering should be reduced to avoid root rot.

FERTILIZER: All Begonias can be fertilized in the spring and summer with a balanced slow-release pellet, or a liquid fertilizer applied every three to four weeks. However, tuberous Begonias should not be fertilized in winter, as they must go dormant to survive.

FLOWERING: Although Begonias display an incredible variety of foliage, they are also cultivated for their showy flowers. Flowering can be promoted by using a fertilizer higher in phosphorus and lower in nitrogen, starting in midsummer.

PROPAGATION: Different propagation strategies can be used on different types of Begonias. Most can be propagated from stem cuttings. Rhizomatous and tuberous Begonias can be propagated from leaf cuttings.

DID YOU KNOW...

· Although Begonias are primarily known for their ornamental uses in the garden and as houseplants, numerous reported ethnobotanical applications exist for different *Begonia* species. These include food, medicine, and even unsubstantiated reports of Begonias being used to polish swords.

· Begonias are mildly toxic to pets and humans.

SCIENTIFIC NAME: *Calathea* spp.
COMMON NAME: Calathea, Zebra Plant, Prayer Plant
FAMILY: Marantaceae

DESCRIPTION: A genus of approximately 60 species of mostly herbaceous perennials reaching up to 1 m in height. They are cultivated for their showy leaves, which grow in clumps on long petioles, and can attain lengths of nearly 0.5 m long. The leaves are typically lanceolate to cordate in shape and green in color, but with attractive variegation and/or leaf venation common on many varieties. The undersides of the leaves are often a reddish color. The flowers are asymmetrical, emerging from spikes of often colorful bracts. At night, the leaves fold up—hence the common name of Prayer Plant.

DISTRIBUTION: It is native to tropical forested habitats of Central and South America.

CULTIVATION AND CARE

LIGHT: Bright to medium indirect

TEMPERATURE: Warm

HUMIDITY: Moderate to high

GROWING MEDIA: Any well-draining potting mix will be adequate for most Calatheas.

WATERING: Plants should be watered moderately during the active growing season of spring and summer and allowed to become slightly dry between waterings. In the dormant winter months, watering should be reduced.

FERTILIZER: Fertilize every two weeks with a balanced indoor plant fertilizer during the spring and summer. It does not require fertilizer during the dormant months.

FLOWERING: *Calathea* is noted for its beautiful foliage, and most cultivars rarely flower indoors.

PROPAGATION: The easiest way to propagate *Calathea* is to divide daughter plants into separate pots during repotting.

DID YOU KNOW...

- Unfurling leaves and inflorescence bracts can hold water, forming shallow "pools" that provide habitat for numerous types of invertebrates.
- *Calathea* spp. is nontoxic to pets and humans.

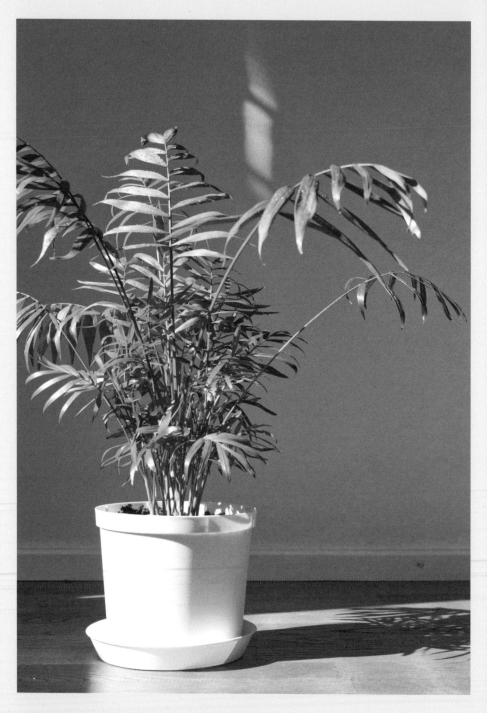

PARLOR PALM, NEANTHE BELLA PALM SEE PAGE 70

SPIDER PLANT, RIBBON PLANT SEE PAGE 72

SCIENTIFIC NAME: *Chamaedorea elegans*
COMMON NAME: Parlor Palm, Neanthe Bella Palm
FAMILY: Arecaceae

DESCRIPTION: A small rhizomatous palm tree, reaching a height of 5 m, although generally remaining under 2 m in height under cultivation. Leaves are pinnate, on long arching stems with up to 40 lanceolate leaflets. Flowers are small, ranging from yellow to dark orange, and are borne in branched clusters.

DISTRIBUTION: It is native to rain forests from southern Mexico to Guatemala.

CULTIVATION AND CARE

LIGHT: Bright to low indirect

TEMPERATURE: Warm to cool

HUMIDITY: Moderate to high

GROWING MEDIA: Any well-draining potting mix will be adequate.

WATERING: The soil should be kept moist during the active growth period of spring and summer. Pots should have good drainage. During the dormant winter period, water less frequently.

FERTILIZER: Fertilize every two weeks with a balanced indoor plant fertilizer during active growth. It does not require fertilizer during the dormant months.

FLOWERING: *Chamaedorea elegans* is favored for its large, pinnate leaves. The flowers are small and not showy.

PROPAGATION: Seed germination is the best propagation strategy.

DID YOU KNOW...

· The leaves of *Chamaedorea elegans* are often used in various decorations because they can survive at least one month after being cut.

· *Chamaedorea elegans* is nontoxic to pets and humans.

SCIENTIFIC NAME: *Chlorophytum comosum*
COMMON NAME: Spider Plant, Ribbon Plant
FAMILY: Asparagaceae

DESCRIPTION: A spreading, herbaceous perennial, with arching, ribbonlike leaves and long, flowering stems reaching up to 1 m in length. The leaves can be up to 50 cm long and 0.5 cm wide. They are naturally solid green in color, but varieties with variegated leaves have been cultured and are the most common types seen in cultivation. Clusters of one to six flowers emerge in intervals along the stems. Individual flowers are approximately 1 cm in width, with six white linear-shaped tepals. The flower clusters also develop plantlets that will root if they touch the soil, forming a new plant.

DISTRIBUTION: It is native to tropical habitats in South Africa, but has been naturalized in several other locations around the world.

CULTIVATION AND CARE

LIGHT: Bright to medium indirect
TEMPERATURE: Warm to cool
HUMIDITY: Low to high

GROWING MEDIA: Any well-draining potting mix will be adequate for most Spider Plants.

WATERING: Water moderately and allow the soil to dry

between waterings. Reduce watering in the winter.

FERTILIZER: Fertilize every four to six weeks with a balanced indoor plant fertilizer during the active growth period of spring and summer. It does not require fertilizer during the dormant winter months.

FLOWERING: Spider Plants will flower freely throughout the growing season.

PROPAGATION: Pot the small offshoots (spiderettes) that arise from the stolons.

DID YOU KNOW...

- The Spider Plant has been used as medicine to treat coughs and improve circulation.
- Studies have shown that the Spider Plant can remove certain toxins from the air. However, it is believed to be insufficient for human health–related concerns, even with many plants in a building.
- Spider Plants are nontoxic to pets and humans.

CROTON SEE PAGE 76

COFFEE PLANT SEE PAGE 78

SCIENTIFIC NAME: *Codiaeum variegatum*
COMMON NAME: Croton
FAMILY: Euphorbiaceae

DESCRIPTION: A bushy evergreen shrub or small tree, up to 3 m in height. The leaves are thick and leathery and generally linear or ovate in shape, and can get up to 30 cm long. The leaves can vary in shape and coloration on the same plant, with some having lobed margins or a curled or twisted form. The leaf color is green, with variegations that change as the plant ages, resulting in a range of leaf colors and combinations on one plant. Variegations either match the leaf venation or appear as random spots or splotches. Flowers are rare in cultivation but consist of tiny flowers in long, axillary racemes.

DISTRIBUTION: It is native from Malaysia and Indonesia to Australia, in scrubby forest habitats.

CULTIVATION AND CARE

LIGHT: Bright indirect

TEMPERATURE: Warm to cool

HUMIDITY: Moderate to high

GROWING MEDIA: Any well-draining potting mix will be adequate.

WATERING: Water moderately in the growing season of spring and summer. Reduce watering during the dormant winter months.

FERTILIZER: Fertilize every four to six weeks with a balanced indoor plant fertilizer during the active growth period. It does not require fertilizer during the dormant months.

FLOWERING: Croton is cultivated for its bright leaves and unique patterns. It occasionally produces insignificant flowers when grown indoors.

PROPAGATION: Woody stems can be rooted to establish new plant starts.

DID YOU KNOW...

- The stems of *Codiaeum variegatum* contain a milky sap that may cause contact dermatitis.
- *Codiaeum variegatum* is mildly toxic to pets and humans.

SCIENTIFIC NAME: *Coffea arabica*
COMMON NAME: Coffee Plant
FAMILY: Rubiaceae

DESCRIPTION: A broadleaf evergreen shrub or small tree that is the source of about 60% of the world's coffee production. In the wild, plants reach heights of up to 12 m, but only up to 2 m when grown indoors. The leaves are opposite in arrangement, elliptical in shape, and colored a dark, glossy green, and are up to 12 cm long and 8 cm wide. The leaf veins are prominent, and the leaf margins are usually undulated. Fragrant, small white flowers, up to 0.25 cm in diameter, are produced in axillary clusters of two to nine. The fruit is a small, fleshy drupe, around 15 mm in diameter, that is dark red when ripe. Each drupe contains two seeds, which are the coffee beans we all know and love.

DISTRIBUTION: It is native to Ethiopia, where it is becoming scarce. However, it is cultivated and has been naturalized in many tropical areas around the world.

CULTIVATION AND CARE

LIGHT: Bright to medium indirect

TEMPERATURE: Warm to cold

HUMIDITY: Moderate to high

GROWING MEDIA: Any commercial, peat-based potting soil will work well for *Coffea arabica.* Adding some additional perlite will improve drainage.

WATERING: *Coffea arabica* plants require copious amounts of water, but care should be taken to ensure the roots don't become waterlogged. A pot with drain holes and soil with good drainage should accompany generous watering.

FERTILIZER: During the spring and summer, liquid fertilizer for acid-loving plants should be applied every two to three weeks.

FLOWERING: Mature plants produce fragrant small, white, star-shaped flowers.

PROPAGATION: Like a few other houseplants, you can propagate *Coffea arabica* from stem cuttings, but cuttings from lateral branches will continue to grow as lateral branches. Cuttings made from a vertical stem will grow into a plant with an upright growth habit.

DID YOU KNOW...

- The ripe fruits are fermented or dried and then roasted to produce various flavors.
- *Coffea arabica* is a tetraploid due to natural hybridization between two other species of *Coffea* that occurred approximately 1 million years ago.
- *Coffea arabica* is toxic to pets and humans.

JADE PLANT SEE PAGE 82

STRING-OF-PEARLS SEE PAGE 84

SCIENTIFIC NAME: *Crassula ovata*
COMMON NAME: Jade Plant
FAMILY: Crassulaceae

DESCRIPTION: A thick-stemmed, branching evergreen shrub up to 2.5 m in height. Stems are green and succulent when young, becoming brown with a woody appearance with age, although never forming actual woody tissue. Stems bear pairs of opposite, roundish, fleshy leaves, mainly near the outer portions of the branch. Leaves can be up to 9 cm long and 4 cm wide. Leaf margins are sharpened and often reddish when growing in sufficient light. Flowers are produced in terminal clusters, bearing several fragrant, star-shaped white- to pink-colored flowers, approximately 15 mm in diameter. They are rarely produced under cultivation.

DISTRIBUTION: It is found on dry, rocky hillsides in South Africa and Mozambique.

CULTIVATION AND CARE

LIGHT: Bright direct

TEMPERATURE: Warm

HUMIDITY: Low to moderate

GROWING MEDIA: Grow *Crassula ovata* in commercial cactus soil, or prepare a mixture of standard potting soil, sand, and perlite. Growing media should be light with good drainage.

WATERING: In the active growing months of spring and summer, water moderately and allow the soil to dry between waterings. In the dormant winter season, reduce watering.

FERTILIZER: Fertilize every four to six weeks with a balanced indoor plant fertilizer during active growth. It does not require fertilizer during the dormant months.

FLOWERING: *Crassula ovata* does not flower regularly. Mature plants are more likely to bloom, but you can encourage flowering by keeping the plant cooler in the evening, taking care not to overwater it, and providing it with bright light during the day.

PROPAGATION: New plant starts can be made from leaf and stem cuttings.

DID YOU KNOW...

- *Crassula ovata* is toxic to dogs, cats, and horses.

SCIENTIFIC NAME: *Curio rowleyanus* (syn. *Senecio rowleyanus*)
COMMON NAME: String-of-Pearls
FAMILY: Asteraceae

DESCRIPTION: A creeping succulent perennial with stems 1 m long that root at the nodes, forming a dense ground cover. It has distinctive modified leaves the size and shape of garden peas, with short stalks. These modified leaves store water, and their size and shape minimize evaporative water loss. The composite flowers are white and rayless and up to 1.5 cm in diameter, with a cinnamon-like aroma.

DISTRIBUTION: It is naturally found in arid habitats of southwest Africa, often in the shade of other plants.

CULTIVATION AND CARE

LIGHT: Bright indirect

TEMPERATURE: Warm to cool

HUMIDITY: Low to high

GROWING MEDIA: Grow in commercial cactus soil, or prepare a mixture of standard potting soil, sand, and perlite. The growing medium should be light with good drainage.

WATERING: In the active growing months of spring and summer, water moderately and allow the soil to dry between waterings. In the dormant winter season, reduce watering.

FERTILIZER: This species does not require a lot of feeding. Fertilize with a diluted balanced fertilizer once or twice during the active growth period. It does not require fertilizer during the dormant months.

FLOWERING: This species will produce small, uniquely fragrant blooms. Typically, it blooms in the summer or early fall, but blooming might occur at any time.

PROPAGATION: New plant starts can be made from stem cuttings.

DID YOU KNOW...

- *Curio* is one of the only succulents in the entire Aster family!
- *Curio rowleyanus* is toxic to pets and humans.

SAGO PALM, KING SAGO SEE PAGE 88

DIEFFENBACHIA, DUMB CANE SEE PAGE 90

SCIENTIFIC NAME: *Cycas revoluta*
COMMON NAME: Sago Palm, King Sago
FAMILY: Cycadaceae

DESCRIPTION: A species of cycad that resembles a palm tree in outward appearance. Young plants are trunkless, appearing as a rosette of leaves emerging directly from the ground. Over time, older leaves die and fall off, leaving a portion of their base behind, ultimately creating a trunk. The growth rate is extremely slow, taking well over 50 or more years to attain a height of around 7 m. Cultivated plants are rarely seen over 1 m in height. The leaves are large and feather-like, reaching up to 2 m in length, and are composed of densely packed, narrow, 10-to-20-cm-long spiny-tipped leaflets. The leaflets are dark green with inrolled (revolute) margins. They are dioecious, with separate male and female plants. The males bear pollen-producing structures called strobili, which are cone-like in appearance. The seed-producing structures on female plants are called megasporophylls, which appear leaflike.

DISTRIBUTION: They are native to southern Japan and southern China, and mainly found near the seashore, in thickets, and on hillsides.

CULTIVATION AND CARE

LIGHT: Bright indirect

TEMPERATURE: Warm day, cool evening

HUMIDITY: Low to moderate

GROWING MEDIA: Cycads do not grow well in heavy, poorly draining soil. A recommended soil mix could contain sand, decomposed granite or gravel, and coir or bark.

WATERING: Water moderately during the spring and summer, ensuring the plant is not sitting in water. Allow the soil to dry between waterings. Reduce watering in the more dormant winter months.

FERTILIZER: Cycads can be sensitive to liquid fertilizers. A slow-release fertilizer pellet can be applied twice during the spring and summer.

FLOWERING: Cycads do not produce flowers.

PROPAGATION: New plants can be initiated from stem or root cuttings.

DID YOU KNOW...

- Cycads are close relatives of pine trees.
- Cycads are toxic to pets and humans.

SCIENTIFIC NAME: *Dieffenbachia* spp.
COMMON NAME: Dieffenbachia, Dumb Cane
FAMILY: Araceae

DESCRIPTION: A genus containing about 50 species of herbaceous perennials. They are generally erect plants with large, simple alternate leaves, broadly elliptical, with prominent pale veins, and often with white speckles or splotches. Most varieties attain heights of 1 to 3 m. As with other plants in the Araceae family, the inflorescence is of the spathe/spadix type.

DISTRIBUTION: They are native to Mexico, the West Indies, and South America, primarily inhabiting rain forest–like habitats.

CULTIVATION AND CARE

LIGHT: Bright to medium indirect

TEMPERATURE: Warm

HUMIDITY: Moderate to high

GROWING MEDIA: Any well-draining potting mix is appropriate.

WATERING: Water moderately during the active growth period of spring and summer. In the winter, reduce watering and allow the soil to dry between waterings.

FERTILIZER: Fertilize every four to six weeks with a balanced indoor plant fertilizer during the active growth period. It does not require fertilizer during the less active winter months.

FLOWERING: *Dieffenbachia* occasionally produces flowers indoors, but it is primarily grown for its attractive foliage.

PROPAGATION: Propagation can be achieved through stem cuttings.

DID YOU KNOW...

- *Dieffenbachia* stems and leaves contain high levels of oxalic acid.
- *Dieffenbachia* is toxic to pets and humans.

DRAGON TREE SEE PAGE 94

LUCKY BAMBOO, RIBBON DRACAENA SEE PAGE 96

SCIENTIFIC NAME: *Dracaena marginata*
COMMON NAME: Dragon Tree
FAMILY: Asparagaceae

DESCRIPTION: A shrub or small tree up to 6 m in height with slender, gray stems that bear diamond-shaped leaf scars when older leaves fall off. The leaves grow in arching clusters at the tip of the stems. They are swordlike in shape, up to 60 cm in length, 1 cm in width, and glossy green, and often have a reddish margin. The flowers are fragrant, tiny, and white, forming round yellow-orange berries.

DISTRIBUTION: It is native to arid habitats on the island of Madagascar.

CULTIVATION AND CARE

LIGHT: Bright to medium indirect

TEMPERATURE: Warm

HUMIDITY: Moderate

GROWING MEDIA: Any well-draining commercial potting soil is sufficient for growth.

WATERING: In the active growing months of spring and summer, water moderately and allow the soil to dry slightly between waterings. In the dormant winter season, reduce watering.

FERTILIZER: Fertilize every four to six weeks with a diluted balanced indoor plant fertilizer when growth is most active. It does not require fertilizer when growth slows or stalls.

FLOWERING: Flowering is unlikely in plants grown indoors.

PROPAGATION: New plants can be started from stem cuttings.

DID YOU KNOW...

· The name *Dracaena* originates from the Greek word drakaina, a female dragon with humanoid features.
· *Dracaena marginata* is toxic to pets and humans.

SCIENTIFIC NAME: *Dracaena sanderiana*

COMMON NAME: Lucky Bamboo,
Ribbon Dracaena

FAMILY: Asparagaceae

DESCRIPTION: An herbaceous perennial with distinctive nodes on upright stems, reminiscent of bamboo. It can attain a height of up to 1.5 m, with widely spaced leaves along the stem. The leaves are lanceolate in shape and slightly twisting, and they reach lengths of nearly 20 cm. They are a soft green, with many cultivars displaying variegation of white or yellow stripes. The flowers are small, white, and not particularly noteworthy.

DISTRIBUTION: It is native to tropical areas of West Africa.

CULTIVATION AND CARE

LIGHT: Bright to medium indirect

TEMPERATURE: Warm

HUMIDITY: Moderate

GROWING MEDIA: Any well-draining commercial potting soil is sufficient for growth. This plant can also be grown in water, although this tends to be for shorter-term periods and is more typically used when it is included in vases and other botanical arrangements. When grown in hydroponic conditions, a layer of rocks should be placed in the bottom of the container to provide a substrate for roots. Plants grown entirely in hydroponic conditions will have a different growth form, with smaller leaves and a more bamboo-like appearance. Water should be replaced weekly.

WATERING: In the active growing period of spring and summer, water moderately and allow the soil to dry slightly between waterings. In the dormant winter season, reduce watering.

FERTILIZER: Fertilize every four to six weeks with a diluted balanced indoor plant fertilizer when growth is most active. It does not require fertilizer when growth slows or stalls.

FLOWERING: Flowering is unlikely in plants grown indoors.

PROPAGATION: New plants can be started from stem cuttings.

DID YOU KNOW...

· Despite looking similar to bamboo and having "bamboo" in its common name, *Dracaena sanderiana* is not closely related to bamboo.

· *Dracaena sanderiana* is toxic to pets and humans.

SNAKE PLANT, MOTHER-IN-LAW'S TONGUE, VIPER'S BOWSTRING HEMP SEE PAGE 100

GOLDEN POTHOS, DEVIL'S IVY, HUNTER'S ROVE SEE PAGE 102

SCIENTIFIC NAME: *Dracaena trifasciata* (syn. *Sansevieria trifasciata*)
COMMON NAME: Snake Plant, Mother-in-Law's Tongue, Viper's Bowstring Hemp
FAMILY: Asparagaceae

DESCRIPTION: A rhizomatous evergreen perennial, forming dense stands of stiffly erect leaves in basal rosettes that grow from the creeping rhizome. In the wild, the leaves can reach up to 1.25 m in height and 6 cm in width, though rarely exceeding half of that size in cultivation. The fleshy leaves are sword shaped and colored dark green, with pale-green, horizontally oriented, irregularly shaped stripes. The flowers are fragrant and appear in dense clusters of greenish-white six-petaled flowers, though rarely occurring on indoor plants. The fruit is an orange berry.

DISTRIBUTION: It is native to tropical areas of West Africa and has been naturalized in other parts of the world.

CULTIVATION AND CARE

LIGHT: Bright to medium indirect

TEMPERATURE: Warm

HUMIDITY: Moderate

GROWING MEDIA: Any well-draining commercial potting soil is sufficient for growth.

WATERING: In the active growing period of spring and summer, water moderately and allow the soil to dry slightly between waterings. In the dormant winter season, reduce watering.

FERTILIZER: Fertilize every four to six weeks with a diluted balanced indoor plant fertilizer when growth is most active. It does not require fertilizer when plant growth slows or stalls.

FLOWERING: Flowering is unlikely in plants grown indoors.

PROPAGATION: New plants can be started from leaf cuttings.

DID YOU KNOW...

- The fibers from *Dracaena trifasciata* are sometimes used to make bowstrings and other products.
- A potted specimen can be seen on the porch in the background of the famous *American Gothic* painting by Grant Wood.
- *Dracaena trifasciata* is toxic to pets and humans.

SCIENTIFIC NAME: *Epipremnum aureum*

COMMON NAME: Golden Pothos, Devil's Ivy, Hunter's Rove

FAMILY: Araceae

DESCRIPTION: An evergreen vine, reaching lengths of up to 20 m, with stems up to 4 cm in diameter. It climbs via aerial roots that can attach to a variety of surfaces. Leaves are alternate in arrangement, with different-shaped juvenile and adult leaves. Juvenile leaves are heart shaped, with entire margins, and up to 20 cm long. Adult leaves are pinnatifid with perforations along the midrib and are up to 1 m long. Leaves are glossy and dark green, with cream to yellow variegation. Trailing stems are often produced, which root in the ground and bear smaller leaves, up to 10 cm long. These are the leaves primarily seen on cultivated specimens. The flower is a cream-colored spathe up to 25 cm long, although, due to a genetic condition, it is rarely, if ever, produced without hormone treatments.

DISTRIBUTION: It is found in tropical forests in Southeast Asia, New Guinea, and northern Australia.

CULTIVATION AND CARE

LIGHT: Bright indirect

TEMPERATURE: Warm

HUMIDITY: Moderate to high

GROWING MEDIA: Any well-draining commercial potting soil is sufficient for growth.

WATERING: This plant should be kept well watered, but overwatering should be avoided to help prevent root rot. Allow the first inch/several centimeters of the soil to dry before each watering.

FERTILIZER: Fertilize every four to six weeks with a diluted indoor plant fertilizer during the active growth period of spring and summer. It does not require fertilizer during the dormant winter months.

FLOWERING: This species produces white, spathe-like flowers, primarily in the summer. It is typically cultivated for its beautiful foliage.

PROPAGATION: It can be easily propagated with stem cuttings.

DID YOU KNOW...

- It is reported to effectively remove indoor organic pollutants, such as formaldehyde and xylene, from the air.
- *Epipremnum aureum* is toxic to pets and humans.

CROWN OF THORNS, CHRIST PLANT SEE PAGE 106

WEEPING FIG, BENJAMIN FIG, INDIAN RUBBER PLANT SEE PAGE 108

SCIENTIFIC NAME: *Euphorbia milii*
COMMON NAME: Crown of Thorns, Christ Plant
FAMILY: Euphorbiaceae

DESCRIPTION: A woody succulent shrub up to 2 m in height in the wild but rarely over 1 m when cultivated. The leaves are fleshy, obovate in shape, and bright green in color, and reach lengths of up to 6 cm. The stems are densely covered by slender spines up to 3 cm long. The actual flowers lack petals and are small and inconspicuous. However, they are subtended by bright red or yellow bracts up to 0.3 cm across, commonly mistaken as petals.

DISTRIBUTION: It is native to Madagascar but has been widely introduced around the world.

CULTIVATION AND CARE

LIGHT: Bright direct or indirect
TEMPERATURE: Warm
HUMIDITY: Low

GROWING MEDIA: Grow in commercial cactus soil, or prepare a mixture of standard potting soil, sand, and perlite. Growing media should be light with good drainage.

WATERING: In the active growing period of early spring to late summer, water moderately and allow the soil to dry between waterings. In the dormant winter season, first reduce watering, then completely stop watering for up to eight weeks.

FERTILIZER: Fertilize every six to eight weeks with a diluted balanced cactus fertilizer during the active growth period. It does not require fertilizer during the dormant months.

FLOWERING: The flowering period for *Euphorbia milii* kept as a houseplant tends to be early fall to winter. Flowering can be encouraged by maintaining the plant in bright light for at least five hours daily.

PROPAGATION: New plants can be started by propagating the new offshoots when repotting mature specimens.

DID YOU KNOW...

· Extracts from the plant are an effective molluscicide.
· *Euphorbia milii* is toxic to pets and humans.

SCIENTIFIC NAME: *Ficus benjamina*

COMMON NAME: Weeping Fig, Benjamin Fig, Indian Rubber Plant

FAMILY: Moraceae

DESCRIPTION: A broadleaf evergreen tree up to 15 m in height, distinguished by its gracefully drooping branches. The leaves are up to 10 cm long, ovate with a pointed tip, and dark green with a glossy appearance. The bark is smooth and generally grayish. The inflorescence is called a syconium, a fleshy, swollen stem with a small opening leading to the interior, where numerous tiny flowers are borne. It is adapted to be pollinated by a particular species of wasp. Wasp pollination is a characteristic shared by all species of fig. It eventually develops into a 2.5 cm–diameter fig.

DISTRIBUTION: It is native to Southeast Asia and Australia, occurring in wet tropical forests. It has become naturalized in the West Indies, Arizona, and Florida.

CULTIVATION AND CARE

LIGHT: Bright indirect

TEMPERATURE: Warm

HUMIDITY: Moderate to high

GROWING MEDIA: Any well-draining commercial potting soil is sufficient for growth.

WATERING: This plant should be kept well watered, but overwatering should be avoided to help prevent root rot. Allow the first inch/several centimeters of the soil to dry before each watering.

FERTILIZER: Fertilize every four to six weeks with a balanced indoor plant fertilizer during the active growth period of spring and summer. Fertilizer can be reduced to once every eight weeks during the winter.

FLOWERING: This species flowers when grown outdoors but only rarely indoors.

PROPAGATION: It can be propagated from stem cuttings.

DID YOU KNOW...

- It is a major indoor allergen, nearly as potent as dust and pet dander.
- *Ficus benjamina* has a toxic sap (latex) that is poisonous to pets and humans.

FIDDLE-LEAF FIG SEE PAGE 112

NERVE PLANT, MOSAIC PLANT SEE PAGE 114

SCIENTIFIC NAME: *Ficus lyrata*
COMMON NAME: Fiddle-Leaf Fig
FAMILY: Moraceae

DESCRIPTION: A broadleaf evergreen tree that can attain a height of up to 30 m in the wild. The Fiddle-Leaf Fig gets its name and is a popular houseplant because of its large, dark-green leaves that are lyrate, or shaped like a fiddle, and that reach lengths of up to 30 cm. In the wild, it produces green figs about 3 cm in diameter. Figs are rarely produced indoors.

DISTRIBUTION: It inhabits rain forests in central and western Africa.

CULTIVATION AND CARE

LIGHT: Bright indirect

TEMPERATURE: Warm

HUMIDITY: Moderate to high

GROWING MEDIA: Any well-draining commercial potting soil is sufficient for growth.

WATERING: This plant should be kept well watered, but overwatering should be avoided to help prevent root rot. Allow the first inch/several centimeters of the soil to dry before each watering.

FERTILIZER: Fertilize every four to six weeks with a balanced

indoor plant fertilizer during the active growth period of spring and summer. Fertilizer can be reduced to once every eight weeks during the winter.

FLOWERING: This species flowers when grown outdoors but only rarely indoors.

PROPAGATION: It can be propagated with stem cuttings.

DID YOU KNOW...

- All figs are pollinated by wasps. The wasp larvae mature inside the fig fruit, with the male wasps spending their entire lives inside.
- *Ficus lyrata* is toxic to pets and humans.

SCIENTIFIC NAME: *Fittonia albivenis*
COMMON NAME: Nerve Plant, Mosaic Plant
FAMILY: Acanthaceae

DESCRIPTION: A low-growing, creeping evergreen perennial, reaching 20 cm in height and spreading about 45 cm. It forms a dense mat of ovate leaves up to 10 cm long. They are dark to olive green and feature veins that are colored white, pink, or red. The inflorescence is a terminal spike up to 8 cm long. The spikes are densely packed with fuzzy bracts, between which the whitish tubular flowers emerge, though they are rarely produced in cultivated plants.

DISTRIBUTION: It is native to tropical rain forests in the northern parts of South America (Brazil, Bolivia, Colombia, Ecuador, and Peru).

CULTIVATION AND CARE

LIGHT: Bright indirect

TEMPERATURE: Warm

HUMIDITY: High

GROWING MEDIA: Any well-draining potting mix will be adequate.

WATERING: Water moderately and allow the soil to dry between waterings. Reduce watering in the dormant winter months.

FERTILIZER: Fertilize every four to six weeks with a diluted balanced indoor plant fertilizer during the active growth period of spring and summer. It does not require fertilizer during the dormant months.

FLOWERING: *Fittonia* does bloom, but flowers are small and insignificant.

PROPAGATION: *Fittonia* can be propagated by stem cuttings.

DID YOU KNOW...

· *Fittonia albivenis* is used medicinally to treat headaches and muscle pain.
· *Fittonia albivenis* is nontoxic to pets and humans.

PEACOCK PLANT, CATHEDRAL WINDOWS SEE PAGE 118

DROOPHEAD TUFTED AIRPLANT, VASE PLANT, SCARLET STAR SEE PAGE 120

SCIENTIFIC NAME: *Goeppertia makoyana*

COMMON NAME: Peacock Plant,
Cathedral Windows

FAMILY: Marantaceae

DESCRIPTION: A clump-forming herbaceous evergreen perennial, up to 0.5 m tall. It has glossy, ovate leaves up to 12 cm long and 7 cm wide. The leaves are generally pale green, with darker green blotches, primarily along the veins. The undersurface of the leaf is a dark purplish red. The new leaves are rolled up when they first emerge. Flowers are spikes of small, tubular white to purple flowers, although they are rarely produced under cultivation.

DISTRIBUTION: It is naturally found in forested habitats of eastern Brazil.

CULTIVATION AND CARE

LIGHT: Bright to medium indirect

TEMPERATURE: Warm

HUMIDITY: Moderate to high

GROWING MEDIA: Any well-draining potting mix will be adequate.

WATERING: Plants should be watered moderately during the active growing season of spring and summer and allowed to become slightly dry between waterings. In the dormant winter period, watering should be reduced.

FERTILIZER: Fertilize every two weeks with a balanced indoor plant fertilizer during the active growth period. It does not require fertilizer during the dormant months.

FLOWERING: *Goeppertia* is noted for its beautiful foliage; most cultivars rarely flower indoors.

PROPAGATION: The easiest way to propagate *Goeppertia* is to divide daughter plants into separate pots during repotting.

DID YOU KNOW...

- The leaf coloration and patterning of *Goeppertia makoyana* act as a defense against butterflies, as they only recognize the darker-colored parts of the leaf, confusing it for a different species and causing them to look elsewhere for a host plant to lay eggs on.
- *Goeppertia makoyana* is nontoxic to pets and humans.

SCIENTIFIC NAME: *Guzmania lingulata*
COMMON NAME: Droophead Tufted Airplant,
Vase Plant, Scarlet Star
FAMILY: Bromeliaceae

DESCRIPTION: An evergreen perennial epiphyte growing in the form of a vase-shaped rosette of leaves. The leaves are strap shaped, extending up to 50 cm above the base, and typically colored dark, glossy green, occasionally with darker stripe-like markings. The flowers are borne in a globular cluster of up to 50 small white or yellowish flowers on a stalk that usually is lower than the leaves. The cluster is surrounded by numerous overlapping leaflike bracts that are brilliantly colored from yellow to red. The flowers will often last for several months, after which the plant forms new offshoots and dies.

DISTRIBUTION: It is found as an epiphyte on trees in tropical rain forests from Mexico to central South America.

CULTIVATION AND CARE

LIGHT: Bright to medium indirect
TEMPERATURE: Warm
HUMIDITY: Moderate to high

GROWING MEDIA: A specialty soil for Bromeliads should be used, or standard potting soil amended with peat and perlite.

WATERING: Plants should be watered moderately during the spring and summer and allowed to become slightly dry between waterings. Ensure the center rosette of bracts remains moist. In the dormant winter period, watering should be reduced.

FERTILIZER: Fertilizer is not required.

FLOWERING: *Guzmania* is noted for its unique foliage and brightly colored floral-like bracts. Tiny flowers are contained inside the center rosette of bracts.

PROPAGATION: *Guzmania* plants produce small "pups" growing off the mother plant. These pups can be carefully excised and grown in separate pots.

DID YOU KNOW...

- It is one of the most popular Bromeliad houseplants worldwide.
- *Guzmania* is nontoxic to pets and humans.

HAWORTHIA SEE PAGE 124

KENTIA PALM, THATCH PALM, PALM COURT PALM SEE PAGE 126

SCIENTIFIC NAME: *Haworthia* spp.
COMMON NAME: Haworthia
FAMILY: Asphodelaceae

DESCRIPTION: A genus of approximately 150 species of small succulents, somewhat similar to *Aloe* in overall form. They form rosettes of thick, fleshy leaves, usually less than 3 cm in diameter, with a few species reaching up to 30 cm in diameter. Most species are stemless and form basal rosettes, but some species grow stems up to 0.5 m in height. The leaves are highly variable between the various species, with an array of leaf thickness and texture, coloration, and markings (or lack thereof) present. Many species have fenestrations, or light windows, on the upper surface of their leaves. Some species grow as solitary individuals, while others can form large clumps over time. The flowers are small, white, and tubular, borne on spikes that can reach up to 0.5 m in height, depending on the species.

DISTRIBUTION: They are native to southern Africa, primarily in the cape of South Africa, where they can be found in a variety of semiarid habitats, such as savannas, thickets, and heathlands, and at a variety of altitudes, in sandy, rocky soils.

CULTIVATION AND CARE

LIGHT: Bright indirect
TEMPERATURE: Warm
HUMIDITY: Low

GROWING MEDIA: Grow in commercial cactus soil, or prepare a mixture of standard potting soil, sand, and perlite. Growing media should be light with good drainage.

WATERING: In the spring and summer, water moderately and allow the soil to dry between waterings. In the dormant winter season, reduce watering.

FERTILIZER: Fertilize once or twice with a diluted balanced indoor plant fertilizer during the active growth period. It does not require fertilizer during the dormant months.

FLOWERING: *Haworthia* species will flower every year after the plants are two to three years old.

PROPAGATION: New plant starts can be made from leaf and stem cuttings.

DID YOU KNOW...

- Some species can withstand freezing temperatures for a short period of time.
- Many species are highly variable themselves, exhibiting different colors based on environmental conditions.
- *Haworthia* is nontoxic to pets and humans.

SCIENTIFIC NAME: *Howea forsteriana*

COMMON NAME: Kentia Palm, Thatch Palm, Palm Court Palm

FAMILY: Arecaceae

DESCRIPTION: A slow-growing palm tree that can reach heights of up to 20 m in the wild. The trunk is narrow (up to 15 cm wide) and ringed by the leaf scars of shed fronds. Up to 36 gracefully arching leaves (fronds) grow from the top of the plant, are pinnate, and are up to 4 m long, with leaflets up to 0.8 m long and 5 cm wide.

DISTRIBUTION: It is native to Lord Howe Island, about 600 km east of Australia's eastern coast. There it can form extensive colonies at low to moderate elevations.

CULTIVATION AND CARE

LIGHT: Bright indirect

TEMPERATURE: Warm

HUMIDITY: Moderate to high

GROWING MEDIA: Any well-draining potting mix will be adequate.

WATERING: The soil should be kept moist during the active growth period of spring and summer. Pots should have good drainage. During the dormant winter period, water less frequently.

FERTILIZER: Fertilize every six to eight weeks with a diluted balanced indoor plant fertilizer during the active growth period. It does not require fertilizer during the dormant months.

FLOWERING: *Howea forsteriana* is favored for its large palm fronds and does not regularly flower indoors.

PROPAGATION: Seed germination is the best propagation strategy.

DID YOU KNOW...

- The first settlers on Lord Howe Island used *Howea forsteriana* to thatch their homes.
- *Howea forsteriana* is one of the world's most popular and widely used houseplants.
- *Howea forsteriana* is nontoxic to pets and humans.

HOYA, WAX PLANT, WAX VINE, PORCELAIN FLOWER SEE PAGE 130

KALANCHOE, CHANDELIER PLANT, MOTHER OF MILLIONS SEE PAGE 132

SCIENTIFIC NAME: *Hoya* spp.
COMMON NAME: Hoya, Wax Plant, Wax Vine, Porcelain Flower
FAMILY: Apocynaceae

DESCRIPTION: A large (500 species) genus of evergreen perennials, most of which are creeping or viny, with other species having a more shrub-like form. The largest species can grow up to 20 m in length or height. The leaves are opposite in arrangement, mostly simple and entire, and often fleshy or succulent. Depending on the species, the leaves may be smooth, hairy, or feltlike and may have white speckles. The flowers are umbellate clusters that emerge from the leaf axils. They are primarily star shaped, with five thick, pointed, waxy-looking petals. They range in diameter from 3 mm to 1 cm. The coloration in most species ranges from white to pink, but some species have yellow, orange, green, or near-black flowers. Many species emit a pleasing aroma and produce copious amounts of nectar.

DISTRIBUTION: They are native to tropical areas of South Asia, Polynesia, New Guinea, and Australia. The various species occupy a broad range of habitats across their range.

CULTIVATION AND CARE

LIGHT: Bright indirect

TEMPERATURE: Warm day, cool evening

HUMIDITY: Low

GROWING MEDIA: Grow in commercial cactus soil, or prepare a mixture of standard potting soil, sand, and perlite. Growing media should be light with good drainage.

WATERING: In the active growing period of spring and summer, water moderately and allow the soil to dry between waterings. In the dormant winter season, reduce watering.

FERTILIZER: Fertilize every four weeks with a balanced indoor plant fertilizer during the active growth period. It does not require fertilizer during the dormant months.

FLOWERING: *Hoya* species will produce a very beautiful and unique inflorescence, but only mature specimens (over five years old) will bloom. Flowering can be encouraged by maintaining the plant in adequate lighting.

PROPAGATION: New plant starts can be made from leaf and stem cuttings.

DID YOU KNOW...

- The common names for *Hoya*, Wax Plant and Porcelain Flower, are in reference to its delicate, waxy flowers.
- *Hoya* is nontoxic to pets and humans.

SCIENTIFIC NAME: *Kalanchoe* spp.

COMMON NAME: Kalanchoe, Chandelier Plant, Mother of Millions

FAMILY: Crassulaceae

DESCRIPTION: A genus of approximately 125 species of perennial succulents. Most species are herbaceous perennials or shrubs. The largest species can get up to 6 m tall, but most are less than 1 m. The leaves tend to be flatter than most succulent genera, and usually have toothed or scalloped margins. They may be smooth and waxy, or covered with a feltlike bloom. Flowers feature four petals that fuse into a tube and are usually borne in umbellate or cyme-like clusters. The various species display a wide range of flower colors. Some species are viviparous, forming plantlets from the leaf edges, which develop into new plants.

DISTRIBUTION: Most species are native to Madagascar and/or tropical parts of western Africa.

CULTIVATION AND CARE

LIGHT: Bright direct or indirect

TEMPERATURE: Warm day, cool evening

HUMIDITY: Low

GROWING MEDIA: Grow in commercial cactus soil, or prepare a mixture of standard potting soil, sand, and perlite. Growing media should be light with good drainage.

WATERING: In the active growing period of spring and summer, water moderately and allow the soil to dry between waterings. In the dormant winter season, reduce watering.

FERTILIZER: Fertilize every four to six weeks with a balanced indoor plant fertilizer during the active growth period. It does not require fertilizer during the dormant months.

FLOWERING: Blooming can be encouraged by maintaining plants in the dark for 12 to 14 hours each evening and in bright light during the day.

PROPAGATION: New plant starts can be made from leaf and stem cuttings.

DID YOU KNOW...

- *Kalanchoe* is adapted from the Chinese kalan chau, which means "that which falls and grows."
- *Kalanchoe* spp. may be toxic to pets and humans.

LIVING STONES SEE PAGE 136

JEWEL ORCHID SEE PAGE 138

SCIENTIFIC NAME: *Lithops* spp.
COMMON NAME: Living Stones
FAMILY: Aizoaceae

DESCRIPTION: A genus of at least 37 species of succulent plants with unique modified leaves. Individual plants consist of only a taproot with two fleshy fused leaves that may only partially emerge above the soil surface, if at all, rarely exceeding 2.5 cm in height. The leaves are primarily thick and bulbous, with a flattened exposed surface. Each leaf is up to 3 cm in diameter, depending on the species. The coloration is variable among the species but tends to be earth tone. The exposed surfaces of the leaves have fenestrations, which allow more light to reach the plant. These fenestrations are variously colored, usually darker than the leaf, and they form various patterns and colors. Exposed leaf surfaces may also be textured to some degree, usually with dimples. These characteristics help the plant survive extremely arid habitats and result in a plant that looks remarkably like a small stone on the ground, blending in with its environment. The camouflage is so effective, it is often difficult for even skilled naturalists to detect them in their natural habitats. Flowers are produced primarily during the fall or winter: small, daisy-like flowers that emerge from between the leaves.

DISTRIBUTION: They are native to arid regions of southern Africa.

CULTIVATION AND CARE

LIGHT: Bright direct

TEMPERATURE: Warm

HUMIDITY: Low

GROWING MEDIA: Grow in commercial cactus soil, or prepare a mixture of standard potting soil, sand, and perlite. Growing media should have good drainage.

WATERING: In the spring and summer, water sparingly and allow the soil to dry between waterings. In the dormant winter season, reduce watering to approximately once a month.

FERTILIZER: Fertilize sparingly, once or twice during the growing season, with a diluted balanced cactus fertilizer. It does not require fertilizer during the dormant months.

FLOWERING: Flowering can be encouraged by keeping plants somewhat cooler, 15.5°C/60°F to 18°C/65°F, during the dormant period. This cactus should also be kept dry for the peak dormant period. Warmer, longer days and moisture will help trigger spring blooming.

DID YOU KNOW...

- Small desert animals eat *Lithops* as a water source, if they can detect them.
- Some species inhabit areas that essentially receive no rainfall and obtain their water from moisture in the air.
- *Lithops* is nontoxic to pets and humans.

SCIENTIFIC NAME: *Ludisia discolor*
COMMON NAME: Jewel Orchid
FAMILY: Orchidaceae

DESCRIPTION: A terrestrial orchid grown more for its leaves than its flowers. The leaves are ovate and range from dark green to maroon, with parallel veins that range from red to white. Flowers are small, white, and orchidlike.

DISTRIBUTION: They can be found in tropical forests across Southeast Asia.

CULTIVATION AND CARE

LIGHT: Bright to medium indirect

TEMPERATURE: Warm

HUMIDITY: High

GROWING MEDIA: The Jewel Orchid is a terrestrial orchid; therefore, it can be grown in a soil-based mix, such as one created for African Violets.

WATERING: Water generously, but do not allow roots to sit in waterlogged conditions. Reduce watering in the dormant winter months.

FERTILIZER: Fertilize every two months with a fertilizer designed for orchids during the active growth period of spring and summer. It does not require fertilizer during the dormant months.

FLOWERING: This plant is primarily grown for its foliage but produces a stalk of flowers in the winter. Plants cultivated in bright, indirect light are more likely to flower when the plant is grown indoors.

PROPAGATION: New plants can be started from stem cuttings.

DID YOU KNOW...

- Unlike most orchids, *Ludisia discolor* is relatively easy to care for and is grown for its unique foliage, not its flowers.
- It has had a convoluted taxonomic history, having been placed in seven different genera over the past 200 years.
- *Ludisia discolor* is nontoxic to pets and humans.

PINCUSHION CACTUS, GLOBE CACTUS, BIRTHDAY CAKE CACTUS SEE PAGE 142

PRAYER PLANT SEE PAGE 144

SCIENTIFIC NAME: *Mammillaria* spp.

COMMON NAME: Pincushion Cactus, Globe Cactus, Birthday Cake Cactus

FAMILY: Cactaceae

DESCRIPTION: One of the largest genera of cacti, with over 200 species and cultivars. *Mammillaria* species are distinguished from other cacti by having cleft areolae, which are the small globular structures from which the spines emerge. Most species tend to be small and globular in shape and covered with variously shaped tubercules that are arranged in a spiral pattern. Most species are no more than 40 cm tall and 20 cm wide. The flowers range up to 7 cm in diameter and usually appear in a ring around the upper surface of the plant. They are composed of numerous lanceolate tepals that may be white, yellow, pink, or red. The fruit is berrylike, juicy, somewhat cylindrical in shape, and may be white, green, pink, or red.

DISTRIBUTION: It is native from Central America to the southern United States, with the greatest number and diversity of species occurring in Mexico.

CULTIVATION AND CARE

LIGHT: Bright direct or indirect

TEMPERATURE: Warm

HUMIDITY: Low

GROWING MEDIA: Grow in commercial cactus soil, or prepare a mixture of standard potting soil, sand, and perlite. Growing media should be light with good drainage.

WATERING: In the active growing period of early spring to late summer, water moderately and allow the soil to dry between waterings. In the dormant season, first reduce watering, then completely stop watering for up to eight weeks in the winter.

FERTILIZER: Fertilize every four to six weeks with a diluted balanced cactus fertilizer during the active growth period. It does not require fertilizer during the dormant months.

FLOWERING: Flowering can be encouraged by keeping plants somewhat cooler, 15.5°C/60°F to 18°C/65°F, during the dormant period. This cactus should also be kept dry for the peak dormant period. Warmer, longer days and moisture will help trigger spring blooming.

PROPAGATION: New plants can be started by propagating the new offshoots when repotting mature specimens.

DID YOU KNOW...

· *Mammillaria* is the most diverse genus in the Cactus family.
· *Mammillaria* is nontoxic to pets and humans.

SCIENTIFIC NAME: *Maranta leuconeura*
COMMON NAME: Prayer Plant
FAMILY: Marantaceae

DESCRIPTION: A rhizomatous clump-forming evergreen perennial, usually no more than 40 cm tall and wide. The leaves are broadly elliptical in shape and up to 15 cm long. The leaves are green with prominent veins, stripes, and blotches in several colors that form eye-catching patterns. The undersurface of the leaves is gray to reddish in coloration. At night, the leaves fold upward; hence the common name. The flowers are small, two lipped, and white in color with small purple spots.

DISTRIBUTION: It is native to tropical rain forests in Brazil.

CULTIVATION AND CARE

LIGHT: Bright indirect

TEMPERATURE: Warm

HUMIDITY: High

GROWING MEDIA: Any well-draining potting soil is adequate.

WATERING: Water generously and allow the soil to dry slightly between waterings during the active growing season of spring and summer. Reduce watering during the dormant winter period.

FERTILIZER: Fertilize every four to six weeks with a balanced

indoor plant fertilizer during the active growth period. It does not require fertilizer during the dormant months.

FLOWERING: This plant is primarily grown for its foliage but produces small flowers. Some growers will remove these flowers to encourage all the plant's energy be dedicated to foliage production.

PROPAGATION: New plants can be started from stem cuttings.

DID YOU KNOW...

- *Maranta* species are closely related to *Calathea* species, and it can be challenging to distinguish between the two genera. Both are nyctinastic, with leaves that fold up in the evening. The *Maranta* species are somewhat easier to care for and propagate.
- *Maranta* is nontoxic to pets and humans.

MONSTERA, SWISS CHEESE PLANT, HURRICANE PLANT SEE PAGE 148

BOSTON FERN, SWORD FERN, FLUFFY RUFFLES SEE PAGE 150

SCIENTIFIC NAME: *Monstera deliciosa*

COMMON NAME: Monstera, Swiss Cheese Plant, Hurricane Plant

FAMILY: Araceae

DESCRIPTION: An evergreen perennial hemiepiphytic vine, meaning it germinates and begins life as an epiphyte, eventually developing roots that reach and grow into the ground. In the wild, they can grow up to 20 m long, reaching up into the canopy of very large trees. As a houseplant, it is rare to see one over 2.5 m. The stems are thick, with long aerial roots. Mature leaves are large, approaching 1 m in length, and are heart shaped, with distinctive perforations and cuts that give them a pinnate appearance. The flower is a 10-to-15-cm-long yellowish spadix partially surrounded by a white spathe.

DISTRIBUTION: It is native to tropical forests from southern Mexico to Panama. It has been widely introduced elsewhere and is becoming invasive in some areas.

CULTIVATION AND CARE

LIGHT: Bright to medium indirect

TEMPERATURE: Warm

HUMIDITY: Moderate to high

GROWING MEDIA: Any well-draining potting soil is adequate.

WATERING: Water generously and allow the soil to dry slightly between waterings during the active growing season of spring and summer. Reduce watering during the dormant winter period.

FERTILIZER: Fertilize every four to six weeks with a balanced indoor plant fertilizer during the active growth period. It does not require fertilizer during the dormant months.

FLOWERING: This plant is primarily grown for its large, unique leaves. *Monstera* does produce flowers in tropical climates.

PROPAGATION: New plants can be started from stem cuttings.

DID YOU KNOW...

- The fruit produced by *Monstera deliciosa* is reported to be a delicious mixture of flavors, including banana, coconut, and pineapple.
- The foliage of this plant is toxic to pets and humans.

SCIENTIFIC NAME: *Nephrolepis exaltata*

COMMON NAME: Boston Fern, Sword Fern, Fluffy Ruffles

FAMILY: Nephrolepidaceae

DESCRIPTION: An evergreen fern that forms a globular cluster of upright, spreading fronds. A mature specimen will be approximately 1 m tall and wide. Individual fronds are sword shaped and can be up to 2 m long and 15 cm wide, with alternately arranged pinnae on either side of the midrib. The pinnae are up to 8 cm long and deltoid shaped, with an asymmetrical base. Sori are produced on the veins on the lower surface of the pinnae and are circular.

DISTRIBUTION: Its native distribution is pantropical, and it can be found in the Americas, Africa, and Polynesia. It inhabits moist, shady locations and can grow both terrestrially and epiphytically.

CULTIVATION AND CARE

LIGHT: Bright to low indirect

TEMPERATURE: Warm to cool

HUMIDITY: Moderate to high

GROWING MEDIA: A commercial soil mix designed for ferns or well-draining soil will be appropriate.

WATERING: Plants should be kept moist but not in standing water. Avoid getting water on the foliage, as brown spots may appear on the leaves.

FERTILIZER: Ferns can be very sensitive to commercial fertilizers. A dilute (quarter-strength) all-purpose indoor plant fertilizer can be used once or twice during the spring and summer.

FLOWERING: Ferns do not produce flowers.

PROPAGATION: Ferns do not produce seeds, but they do produce spores contained in sori found along the undersurfaces of the leaves. The spores can be germinated using the techniques described earlier in this book. The easiest method of propagating new Boston Ferns is to divide them in the dormant growth period in the winter, ensuring each division contains ample roots, rhizomes, and foliage.

DID YOU KNOW...

· The Boston Fern was named to recognize its commercial origin when it was discovered as a fern variant shipped from Philadelphia to Boston in the early nineteenth century.
· Boston Ferns are nontoxic to pets and humans.

FALSE SHAMROCK SEE PAGE 154

MONEY TREE, GUIANA CHESTNUT, WATER CHESTNUT, PROVISION TREE, SABA NUT SEE PAGE 156

SCIENTIFIC NAME: *Oxalis triangularis*
COMMON NAME: False Shamrock
FAMILY: Oxalidaceae

DESCRIPTION: An herbaceous rhizomatous perennial up to 50 cm tall and wide. It does not have a stem per se but rather a cluster of leaves on long petioles that emerge from a scaly tuberous rhizome that is usually at or below ground level. The leaves are compound, with three broad, triangular leaflets typically held perpendicular to the petiole, superficially resembling a clover leaf. In the wild, the leaves are green, but cultivars featuring purple leaves have been developed. The flowers are borne on long stalks and are white, with five ovate petals.

DISTRIBUTION: It is native to South America, from Brazil to Argentina, where it can be found along the banks of rocky streams. It has also become adventive in India and the United States, with reports from Arkansas, Louisiana, and Florida.

CULTIVATION AND CARE

LIGHT: Bright to low indirect

TEMPERATURE: Warm to cool

HUMIDITY: Low to high

GROWING MEDIA: Any well-draining potting soil is adequate.

WATERING: Water moderately and allow the soil to dry slightly between waterings. Take care not to overwater or underwater during the active growing period of spring and summer. Reduce watering in the dormant winter period.

FERTILIZER: Fertilize every four to six weeks with a balanced indoor plant fertilizer during the active growth period. It does not require fertilizer during the dormant months.

FLOWERING: This plant is primarily grown for its shamrock-shaped foliage but produces showy white to purple flowers in the spring.

PROPAGATION: New plants can be propagated by dividing the bulbs in the dormant period.

DID YOU KNOW...

- *Oxalis* is nyctinastic; its leaves fold up during the evening or when the plant is in the dark for an extended period.
- It is surprisingly hardy and can withstand temperatures down to –12°C/10°F.
- *Oxalis* is toxic or mildly toxic to pets and humans.

SCIENTIFIC NAME: *Pachira aquatica*

COMMON NAME: Money Tree, Guiana Chestnut, Water Chestnut, Provision Tree, Saba Nut

FAMILY: Malvaceae

DESCRIPTION: A broadleaf evergreen tree reaching heights of up to 20 m in the wild (less than 10 m in cultivation). It features palmately compound leaves with five to nine lanceolate leaflets 10 cm to 25 cm long and shiny green. Flowers (rarely seen in cultivation) are five parted and pale green to cream in color, with very narrow, strap-shaped petals that can reach 30 cm in length, making them one of the largest tree flowers on Earth. The fruit is a woody capsule that reaches lengths of up to 30 cm and that contains edible nutlike seeds.

DISTRIBUTION: It is native to tropical rain forests from Mexico to northern South America, mostly found in freshwater swamps and estuarine wetlands.

CULTIVATION AND CARE

LIGHT: Bright to low indirect

TEMPERATURE: Warm to cool

HUMIDITY: Moderate to high

GROWING MEDIA: Any well-draining potting soil is adequate.

WATERING: Water moderately and allow the soil to dry between waterings. Reduce watering during the dormant winter period.

FERTILIZER: Fertilize every four to six weeks with a balanced indoor plant fertilizer during the active growth period of spring and summer. It does not require fertilizer during the dormant months.

FLOWERING: This plant is primarily grown for its foliage, but it produces beautiful flowers outdoors in the appropriate climate.

PROPAGATION: The Money Tree can be propagated from stem cuttings.

DID YOU KNOW...

- *Pachira aquatica* acquired its common name Money Tree after a legend about a man who prayed for money, was gifted this tree, and made his fortune selling its seeds.
- It is believed to bring luck and wealth to the home.
- *Pachira aquatica* is nontoxic to pets and humans.

BABY RUBBER PLANT, PEPPER FACE SEE PAGE 160

HEART-LEAF PHILODENDRON SEE PAGE 162

SCIENTIFIC NAME: *Peperomia obtusifolia*
COMMON NAME: Baby Rubber Plant, Pepper Face
FAMILY: Piperaceae

DESCRIPTION: A small, bushy herbaceous perennial, up to 30 cm tall and wide. The thick stems bear elliptical leaves up to 15 cm long that are thick, waxy, and colored dark green, often with paler variegations. The flowers are not showy and do not look like flowers. They resemble long, thin, pale-green stalks and are rarely produced in cultivation.

DISTRIBUTION: It is native to Florida, Mexico, and the Caribbean, where it is often found as an epiphyte in rain forest habitats.

CULTIVATION AND CARE

LIGHT: Bright to low indirect

TEMPERATURE: Warm to cool

HUMIDITY: Moderate to high

GROWING MEDIA: Any well-draining potting soil is adequate.

WATERING: Water moderately and allow the soil to dry between waterings. Reduce watering during the dormant winter period.

FERTILIZER: Fertilize every four to six weeks with a balanced indoor plant fertilizer during the active growth period of spring and summer. It does not require fertilizer during the dormant months.

FLOWERING: This plant is primarily grown for its foliage but produces nonshowy flowers.

PROPAGATION: Stem cuttings can be used to propagate new plants.

DID YOU KNOW...

- *Peperomia* is closely related to the black pepper plant.
- *Peperomia obtusifolia* is nontoxic to pets and humans.

SCIENTIFIC NAME: *Philodendron hederaceum*
COMMON NAME: Heart-Leaf Philodendron
FAMILY: Araceae

DESCRIPTION: An evergreen epiphytic vine that reaches lengths of up to 6 m in the wild but rarely over 1 m in cultivation. It has large (up to 30 cm long) heart-shaped leaves colored a glossy dark green. The flowers are typical Arum-type flowers with a greenish-white spathe/spadix. They are infrequently produced on mature cultivated specimens.

DISTRIBUTION: It is native to Mexico, Brazil, and the West Indies, where it is commonly found growing in the canopy of tropical rain forests.

CULTIVATION AND CARE

LIGHT: Bright indirect
TEMPERATURE: Warm
HUMIDITY: High

GROWING MEDIA: It will thrive in various soil mixes but performs best in a light, well-aerated mix with good drainage.

WATERING: The soil should be kept moist during the active growth period of spring and summer. Allow the top inch/several centimeters of the soil to dry before watering again. Pots should have good drainage. Bottom watering is best. During the dormant winter period, water less frequently.

FERTILIZER: Fertilize the plant every four to six weeks with a slow-release indoor plant fertilizer during the spring and summer.

FLOWERING: Philodendrons are typically grown for their foliage and rarely flower indoors.

PROPAGATION: New plants can be started from stem cuttings.

DID YOU KNOW...

- *Philodendron hederaceum* can be grown potted in soil or like an epiphyte, growing on other plants and structures for support.
- Many *Philodendron* growers use a pole covered in moss to provide a structure for plant growth.
- *Philodendron* is toxic or mildly toxic to pets and humans.

CHINESE MONEY PLANT, PANCAKE PLANT, UFO PLANT SEE PAGE 166

STAGHORN FERN, ELKHORN FERN SEE PAGE 168

SCIENTIFIC NAME: *Pilea peperomioides*

COMMON NAME: Chinese Money Plant,
Pancake Plant, UFO Plant

FAMILY: Urticaceae

DESCRIPTION: An evergreen perennial with an upright, unbranched stem up to 30 cm tall. The leaves are circular and up to 10 cm in diameter. Its inconspicuous flowers are similar to nettles. They are borne on long petioles that grow outward in all directions from the stem and attach to the leaf near its center.

DISTRIBUTION: It is native to China and mainly grows on rocks in damp, shady forests.

CULTIVATION AND CARE

LIGHT: Medium indirect

TEMPERATURE: Warm

HUMIDITY: Moderate to high

GROWING MEDIA: Any well-draining commercial potting soil is sufficient for growth.

WATERING: In the active growing period of spring and summer, water moderately and allow the soil to dry slightly between waterings. In the dormant winter season, reduce watering.

FERTILIZER: Fertilize every four to six weeks with a balanced

indoor plant fertilizer during the active growth period. It does not require fertilizer during the dormant months.

FLOWERING: Flowering is unlikely in plants grown indoors.

PROPAGATION: New plants can be started from the young "pups" that arise from the base of the mother plant. These can be carefully removed from the mother plant and potted as new plants.

DID YOU KNOW...

- This plant is believed to symbolize wealth and good luck and is referred to as the Chinese Money Plant because the round leaves look like stacks of coins.
- *Pilea peperomioides* is nontoxic to pets and humans.

SCIENTIFIC NAME: *Platycerium* spp.
COMMON NAME: Staghorn Fern, Elkhorn Fern
FAMILY: Polypodiaceae

DESCRIPTION: A group of 18 species of evergreen epiphytic ferns with distinctive fronds. Two types of fronds are produced. Sterile fronds, which are small and shield-shaped, grow at the base of the fern and are usually appressed against the tree. Their purpose is to shield the small root system. Fertile fronds are much larger (up to 1 m) and leathery, and they branch dichotomously. The branching pattern, combined with the feltlike appearance of the fertile fronds, is the reason for the common names, as it resembles the antlers of deer and elk.

DISTRIBUTION: The 18 species are spread out in tropical and subtropical areas of South America, Africa, Asia, and Australia.

CULTIVATION AND CARE

LIGHT: Bright indirect

TEMPERATURE: Warm

HUMIDITY: Moderate to high

GROWING MEDIA: This plant is an epiphyte, and in nature will be found growing on other plants and structures for support. The Staghorn Fern can be mounted on wood pieces or in hanging baskets, with the root ball covered with moss to maintain moisture and improve aesthetics.

WATERING: The root ball should be kept moist but not drenched or left in standing water.

FERTILIZER: Fertilize every four to six weeks with a diluted balanced indoor plant fertilizer during the active growth period from early spring to late summer. It does not require fertilizer during the dormant winter months.

FLOWERING: Ferns do not produce flowers.

PROPAGATION: The Staghorn Fern can be started from spores located in sori on the underside of leaves, but this is a time-intensive process. The plant can be cut in half during the active growing season in spring and summer, and each division remounted. It also produces small "pups" that grow off the shield fronds. These are young plants that can be carefully removed and maintained in sphagnum moss until they increase in size.

DID YOU KNOW...

- Like all ferns, the Staghorn Fern does not produce flowers or seeds.
- *Platycerium* spp. is nontoxic to pets and humans.

MISTLETOE CACTUS SEE PAGE 172

DWARF UMBRELLA TREE, PARASOL PLANT SEE PAGE 174

SCIENTIFIC NAME: *Rhipsalis baccifera*
COMMON NAME: Mistletoe Cactus
FAMILY: Cactaceae

DESCRIPTION: An epiphytic cactus that is very un-cactus-like, forming large, dense clusters of hanging stems. The stems may reach up to 9 m in length, although they rarely exceed 4 m. The stems are thin (0.5 cm), cylindrical, jointed, and freely branching. They are mostly green or pale green; unlike most cacti, they lack spines. Bristly areoles may be present on young shoots, but they fall off over time. Solitary flowers are often produced abundantly along the stems. They are white to greenish, radially symmetrical, and smaller than 1 cm in diameter. They form spherical berries up to 1 cm in diameter that may be white, pink, or red.

DISTRIBUTION: It has a broad native range, from Central and South America to tropical parts of Africa and Sri Lanka.

CULTIVATION AND CARE

LIGHT: Bright indirect

TEMPERATURE: Warm

HUMIDITY: Moderate to high

GROWING MEDIA: Grow in commercial cactus soil, or prepare a mixture of standard potting soil, sand, and perlite. Growing media should be light with good drainage.

WATERING: In the active growing period of early spring to late summer, water moderately and allow the soil to dry between waterings. In the dormant winter season, reduce watering.

FERTILIZER: Fertilize every four to six weeks with a diluted balanced cactus fertilizer during the active growth period. It does not require fertilizer during the dormant months.

FLOWERING: Flowering can be encouraged by keeping plants somewhat cooler, 15.5°C/60°F to 18°C/65°F, during the dormant period. Flowering often occurs in late winter to early spring.

PROPAGATION: New plant starts can be made from leaf and stem cuttings.

DID YOU KNOW...

- *Rhipsalis baccifera* has a mysterious distribution! It is the only cactus species naturally found outside the Western Hemisphere.
- *Rhipsalis* is nontoxic to pets and humans.

SCIENTIFIC NAME: *Heptapleurum arboricola* (syn. *Schefflera arboricola*)
COMMON NAME: Dwarf Umbrella Tree, Parasol Plant
FAMILY: Araliaceae

DESCRIPTION: A broadleaf evergreen shrub up to 9 m in height. While mostly growing as an upright terrestrial tree, it occasionally grows as an epiphyte on other trees. It has palmately compound leaves, with seven to nine elliptical leaflets up to 20 cm long and 10 cm wide. The leaves are shiny and green and have a leathery texture. Numerous tiny, five-parted red flowers are borne in panicles. The fruit is a small drupe that changes from orange to black as it ripens.

DISTRIBUTION: It is native to Taiwan and the Chinese island of Hainan, where it is found scrambling up trees in tropical rain forests.

CULTIVATION AND CARE

LIGHT: Bright to medium indirect

TEMPERATURE: Warm

HUMIDITY: Moderate to high

GROWING MEDIA: Any well-draining commercial potting soil is sufficient for growth.

WATERING: In the active growing period of spring and

summer, water moderately and allow the soil to dry slightly between waterings. In the dormant winter season, reduce watering.

FERTILIZER: Fertilize every four to six weeks with a balanced indoor plant fertilizer during the active growth period. It does not require fertilizer during the dormant months.

FLOWERING: Flowering is unlikely in plants grown indoors.

PROPAGATION: New plants can be started from stem cuttings.

DID YOU KNOW...

· *Heptapleurum arboricola* is toxic to pets and humans.

CHRISTMAS CACTUS, THANKSGIVING CACTUS SEE PAGE 178

SILVER VINE, SILVER SATIN, SATIN POTHOS SEE PAGE 180

SCIENTIFIC NAME: *Schlumbergera* spp.
COMMON NAME: Christmas Cactus, Thanksgiving Cactus, others
FAMILY: Cactaceae

DESCRIPTION: A genus of around 10 species of mostly epiphytic cacti. They lack true leaves, instead forming cladodes, flattened, segmented stems or branches that perform the same functions as leaves. The edges of the cladodes may be toothed or have small spines. The terminal flowers are showy, with 20 to 30 tepals that can be white, yellow, orange, red, pink, or purple.

DISTRIBUTION: They are native to the coastal mountains of Brazil, in habitats that are much shadier and wetter than most other cacti.

CULTIVATION AND CARE

LIGHT: Bright indirect

TEMPERATURE: Warm

HUMIDITY: Low

GROWING MEDIA: Grow in commercial cactus soil, or prepare a mixture of standard potting soil, sand, and perlite. Growing media should be light with good drainage.

WATERING: In the active growing period of early spring to late summer, water moderately and allow the soil to dry between waterings. In the dormant winter season, reduce watering.

FERTILIZER: Fertilize every four to six weeks with a diluted balanced indoor plant fertilizer during the active growth period. It does not require fertilizer during the dormant months.

FLOWERING: This species produces showy, colorful blooms at the end of its stems during the late fall and winter. Flowering can be encouraged by placing the plant in complete darkness for a minimum of 12 hours per night and in bright, indirect light during the day for two months before the desired winter flowering time.

PROPAGATION: New plant starts can be made from leaf and stem cuttings.

DID YOU KNOW...

- Many commercially grown "Christmas Cactus" plants are really the Thanksgiving Cactus, a different species with a subtly different leaf shape and plant form.
- *Schlumbergera* spp. is nontoxic to pets and humans.

SCIENTIFIC NAME: *Scindapsus pictus*

COMMON NAME: Silver Vine, Silver Satin, Satin Pothos

FAMILY: Araceae

DESCRIPTION: An evergreen vine growing up to 3 m in length, producing two distinct kinds of leaves over its life span (juvenile and mature). Cultivated plants are primarily grown in the juvenile phase, with leaves that are cordate in shape with entire margins, reaching lengths up to 10 cm long. Mature leaves are pinnately lobed. The leaves have a satiny texture and are matte green, with prominent, irregularly shaped silver blotches. Flowers are small and inconspicuous and rarely produced when cultivated.

DISTRIBUTION: It is native to tropical areas of Southeast Asia, where it is chiefly seen climbing up various trees.

CULTIVATION AND CARE

LIGHT: Bright indirect

TEMPERATURE: Warm

HUMIDITY: Moderate to high

GROWING MEDIA: Any well-draining commercial potting soil is sufficient for growth.

WATERING: This plant should be kept well watered, but overwatering should be avoided to help prevent root rot. Allow the first inch/several centimeters of the soil to dry before each watering.

FERTILIZER: Fertilize every four to six weeks with a diluted indoor plant fertilizer during the active growth period of spring and summer. It does not require fertilizer during the dormant winter months.

FLOWERING: This species produces white spathe-like flowers, primarily in the summer. However, it is typically cultivated for its beautiful foliage.

PROPAGATION: It can be easily propagated from stem cuttings.

DID YOU KNOW...

· *Scindapsus pictus* is moderately toxic to pets and humans, due to the oxalic acid it contains.

DONKEY TAIL SEE PAGE 184

PEACE LILY, SPATH FLOWER, WHITE SAILS SEE PAGE 186

SCIENTIFIC NAME: *Sedum morganianum*
COMMON NAME: Donkey Tail
FAMILY: Crassulaceae

DESCRIPTION: A succulent perennial with creeping or trailing stems up to 1 m in length. The thick, fleshy leaves are small and cylindrical, with a pointed tip. They have a smooth texture, are bluish green, and are covered by a whitish bloom. They grow in dense, overlapping whorls, completely hiding the stem. During wet weather, the leaves swell up. Conversely, they shrivel during dry spells. Pink flowers with five pointed petals are borne in terminal clusters of one to six.

DISTRIBUTION: It is native to southern Mexico and Honduras and can be found in rocky, arid habitats.

CULTIVATION AND CARE

LIGHT: Bright direct or indirect

TEMPERATURE: Warm day, cool evening

HUMIDITY: Low

GROWING MEDIA: Grow in commercial cactus soil, or prepare a mixture of standard potting soil, sand, and perlite. Growing media should be light with good drainage.

WATERING: In the active growing period of spring and summer, water moderately and allow the soil to dry between waterings. In the dormant winter season, reduce watering.

FERTILIZER: Fertilize every four to six weeks with a balanced indoor plant fertilizer during the active growth period. It does not require fertilizer during the dormant months.

FLOWERING: This species will produce small, bright-pink blooms at the end of stems but does not flower regularly.

PROPAGATION: New plant starts can be made from leaf and stem cuttings.

DID YOU KNOW...

· All *Sedum* species are nontoxic to pets and humans and are edible, although some should be cooked before consumption.

SCIENTIFIC NAME: *Spathiphyllum* spp.

COMMON NAME: Peace Lily, Spath Flower, White Sails

FAMILY: Araceae

DESCRIPTION: A genus of approximately 50 species of clump-forming evergreen perennials. They grow up to 2 m tall in their natural habitat, but cultivated specimens rarely exceed 1 m. The leaves are lanceolate in shape and up to 70 cm long and 30 cm wide, and they have erect petioles about equally as long. They are dark, glossy green with prominently indented veins. The flower is a greenish spadix with a whitish spathe. They are long-lasting and are produced year-round.

DISTRIBUTION: They are native to Central America and Southeast Asia, and are primarily found growing in tropical forests.

CULTIVATION AND CARE

LIGHT: Bright indirect

TEMPERATURE: Warm to cool

HUMIDITY: Low to high

GROWING MEDIA: Any well-draining potting mix is adequate.

WATERING: Water moderately and allow the soil to dry between waterings. Reduce watering during the dormant winter season.

FERTILIZER: Fertilize every four to six weeks with a balanced indoor plant fertilizer during the active growth period of spring and summer. It does not require fertilizer during the dormant months.

FLOWERING: This species is known for its elegant flowers. Blooming usually occurs in the spring, but in mature specimens a second bloom may occur in the autumn. Flowering can be encouraged by ensuring plants receive adequate lighting.

PROPAGATION: Plants can be repotted and divided every two to three years. Ensure that each division includes roots and basal shoots. Propagation from stem or leaf cuttings is not possible.

DID YOU KNOW...

- This plant is referred to as the Peace Lily because its showy white flowers are reminiscent of a white flag, the universal symbol of peace.
- The sap is an irritant. Ingestion may cause stomach upset.
- *Spathiphyllum* spp. is mildly toxic to pets and humans.

WANDERING PLANT, WANDERING DUDE, INCH PLANT SEE PAGE 190

SILVER DOLLAR VINE, PENNY PLANT SEE PAGE 192

SCIENTIFIC NAME: *Tradescantia zebrina*

COMMON NAME: Wandering Plant, Wandering Dude, Inch Plant

FAMILY: Commelinaceae

DESCRIPTION: An herbaceous trailing evergreen up to 15 cm tall and 60 cm wide. The creeping stems root at the nodes, forming a dense, ground-covering mat. The fleshy leaves are ovate with a pointed tip and a clasping base up to 6 cm in length. They are approximately 1 in/2.5 cm apart along the stem; hence the common name Inch Plant. They are bluish green, with two whitish stripes parallel to the midvein (one on each side). The flowers are small and have three purplish petals.

DISTRIBUTION: It is native from Mexico to northern South America and found in various moist habitats.

CULTIVATION AND CARE

LIGHT: Bright to low indirect

TEMPERATURE: Warm to cool

HUMIDITY: Moderate to high

GROWING MEDIA: Any well-draining potting mix is adequate.

WATERING: Water moderately and allow the soil to dry between waterings. Reduce watering during the dormant winter season.

FERTILIZER: Fertilize every four to six weeks with a balanced indoor plant fertilizer during the active growth period of spring and summer. It does not require fertilizer during the dormant months.

FLOWERING: *Tradescantia zebrina* will flower throughout the growing season.

PROPAGATION: It can be propagated from stem cuttings.

DID YOU KNOW...

- Many plant lovers may recognize this beautiful houseplant and refer to it by an outdated common name, which has its origins in apocryphal mythology with anti-Semitic connotations. For this reason, all growers should adopt either the scientific name or the newly proposed common names (Wandering Plant, Wandering Dude, Inch Plant) for this plant.
- *Tradescantia zebrina* is nontoxic to pets and humans.

SCIENTIFIC NAME: *Xerosicyos danguyi*
COMMON NAME: Silver Dollar Vine, Penny Plant
FAMILY: Cucurbitaceae

DESCRIPTION: A succulent perennial vine that can climb up to 5 m in height. The stems are thin and branching, with small bifurcate tendrils that curl around surrounding vegetation and facilitate the vine's upward and outward growth. The leaves are fleshy and thick, broadly ovate to nearly circular, and up to 4 cm long and 3.5 cm wide. The leaf coloration ranges from grayish green to bluish green. The flowers are small and yellowish green, borne in umbellate clusters from the leaf axils. The fruit is a broadly conical capsule about 3 cm long, containing four elliptical seeds.

DISTRIBUTION: It is native to Madagascar, where it inhabits dry forests and shrublands.

CULTIVATION AND CARE

LIGHT: Bright direct or indirect

TEMPERATURE: Warm day, cool evening

HUMIDITY: Low

GROWING MEDIA: Grow in commercial cactus soil, or prepare a mixture of standard potting soil, sand, and perlite. Growing media should be light with good drainage.

WATERING: In the active growing period of spring and

summer, water moderately and allow the soil to dry between waterings. In the dormant winter season, reduce watering. Note that this species is not as susceptible to root rot as other succulents and can be maintained with a little more moisture than other species.

FERTILIZER: Fertilize every four to six weeks with a balanced indoor plant fertilizer during the active growth period. It does not require fertilizer during the dormant months.

FLOWERING: It is a dioecious plant, which means that separate male and female flowers are produced on different plants. In this species, flowering occurs in the spring.

PROPAGATION: This species can be easily propagated from stem cuttings. Plants started from stem cuttings will not have a large caudex like those grown from seed.

DID YOU KNOW...

· This unique plant belongs to the same family as cucumbers and watermelons!

· *Xerosicyos danguyi* is nontoxic to pets and humans.

ZZ PLANT, ZANZIBAR GEM, ETERNITY PLANT SEE PAGE 196

SCIENTIFIC NAME: *Zamioculcas zamiifolia*

COMMON NAME: ZZ Plant, Zanzibar Gem, Eternity Plant

FAMILY: Araceae

DESCRIPTION: A stemless semievergreen perennial with large potato-like rhizomes. Emerging from the rhizomes are thick, arching, pinnately compound leaves that reach up to 1 m in length, with six to eight pairs of leaflets. Leaflets are alternately arranged and ovate in shape with a pointed tip (acuminate), and they range from 2 cm to 8 cm in length. The leaflets are thick and waxy, imparting a shiny appearance. They are mostly dark green, with new growth often having more of a lime green color. Several cultivars have been bred, including giant and dwarf varieties, varieties with more spherical leaves, and varieties with leaves variegated with white or gold. Flowers are small spathes in a 5-cm-to-7-cm-long spadix, typically bright yellow to bronze in color.

DISTRIBUTION: It is naturally found in dry forest and grassland habitats in eastern and southern Africa.

CULTIVATION AND CARE

LIGHT: Bright to low indirect

TEMPERATURE: Warm to cool

HUMIDITY: Low to moderate

GROWING MEDIA: Performs best in a light, well-aerated mix with good drainage.

WATERING: During the spring and summer, it should be watered sparingly and allowed to dry out between waterings. Watering should be reduced in the dormant winter months.

FERTILIZER: These plants do not require a lot of fertilizer. One application of a diluted indoor houseplant fertilizer in the spring is sufficient.

FLOWERING: This plant rarely produces flowers and is known for its unique and beautiful foliage.

PROPAGATION: It can be propagated from leaf cuttings. Ensure that the petiole is included in the excised plant material you will use for propagation. Plant the leaves with the petiole buried in 1 cm to 2 cm of potting mix with good drainage. Patience is required to propagate this species, as it can take up to six months for new rhizomes to form on leaf cuttings.

DID YOU KNOW...

- With its slow growth rate and thick, waxy leaves, *Zamioculcas zamiifolia* is often mistaken for an artificial plant.
- While it is usually listed as "toxic," it is only an irritant due to the calcium oxalate crystals contained in all parts of the plant.

TABLE 1			
	BRIGHT (*can tolerate direct light)	**MEDIUM**	**LOW**
DRY (water sparingly)	*Aloe vera** *Beaucarnea recurvata* *Crassula ovata** *Curio rowleyanus* *Euphorbia milii** *Haworthia* spp. *Hoya* spp. *Kalanchoe* spp.* *Lithops* spp.* *Mammillaria* spp.* *Rhipsalis baccifera* *Schlumbergera* spp. *Sedum morganianum** *Xerosicyos danguyi**	*Pilea peperomioides*	*Aspidistra elatior*

Table 1. A matrix of soil moisture and lighting conditions for the houseplants included in this book.

TABLE 1

	BRIGHT (*can tolerate direct light)	MEDIUM	LOW
MODERATE (allow to dry between waterings)	Alocasia spp. Begonia spp. Codiaeum variegatum Cycas revoluta Epipremnum aureum Ficus spp. Pachira aquatica Scindapsus pictus Tradescantia zebrina	Aeschynanthus radicans Calathea spp. Chlorophytum comosum Dieffenbachia spp. Dracaena spp. Fittonia albivenis Goeppertia makoyana Heptapleurum arboricola Howea forsteriana Maranta leuconeura Monstera deliciosa Spathiphyllum spp.	Aglaonema spp. Chamaedorea elegans Oxalis triangularis Peperomia obtusifolia
HIGH (keep the soil moist, not saturated)	Anthurium andraeanum* Araucaria heterophylla Philodendron hederaceum Platycerium spp.	Asparagus setaceus Asplenium nidus Coffea arabica Guzmania lingulata Ludisia discolor	Nephrolepis exaltata

TABLE   199

GLOSSARY

Anoxic – Lacking oxygen.

Areolae – In cacti, they are the bump-like structures from which spines grow.

Axillary – In botany it refers to the leaf axil—the point on the stem where the leaf attaches.

Cladode – A flattened stem that replaces and serves the same function as leaves.

Coir – Coconut fiber extracted from the husk.

Composite – The type of flower in the Asteraceae family that is composed of a dense cluster of tiny flowers (florets) that superficially resemble a single flower. Daisies and sunflowers are examples.

Conifer – A type of plant that produces seeds in a cone-like structure called a strobilus and narrow, needlelike leaves. Pines and spruces are examples.

Cordate – A leaf that is heart shaped.

Corm – A small, swollen portion of a plant stem that is underground, and that is used as an energy/nutrient reserve.

Cultivar – A particular variety of a plant species that has desirable attributes or traits. In order to retain these traits, they can only be propagated asexually (division, grafting, tissue culture, etc.), or through very controlled breeding.

Cyme – A type of flower arrangement where the main stem initially produces one terminal flower, followed by a succession of additional flowers produced on lateral branches off the main stem. The terminal flower is the first to open.

Drupe – A fruit type distinguished by containing a seed covered by a hard, stony pit surrounded by a fleshy outer layer. Cherries, plums, and almonds are all examples of drupes.

Elliptical – A leaf shape characterized by having an oval-shaped leaf, wider at the base and tapered near the top. Leaves of this shape are about twice as long as they are wide.

Epiphyte – An organism that grows on a plant for support only, and does not otherwise parasitize the plant.

Fenestration – An arrangement of small perforations or transparent areas on plant structures (primarily leaves).

Hybrid – A plant that is the result of the pollination of one plant by another plant that is in a different taxonomic group, whether it be genus, species, variety, etc.

Lanceolate – A leaf shape characterized by being about four times longer than wide and tapering to a point at the end.

Lumen – A unit of measurement of the amount of visible light emitted from a source.

Lux – A unit of measurement of the amount of visible light in a certain area. One lux is equal to one lumen per square meter.

Lyrate – Shaped like a lyre.

Margin – The edge of a structure, mostly used when describing leaves.

Midrib – The central vein of a leaf, from which all other veins arise.

Node – On a plant stem, the region where new leaves, stems, or buds will emerge.

Obovate – Egg shaped, with the basal end narrower than the tip.

Ovate – Egg shaped, with the basal end wider than the tip.

Palmate leaf – A leaf that is subdivided into leaflets that radiate from a common point.

Panicle – An inflorescence type characterized by flowers loosely arranged in a spike with many branches.

Peat – Partially decayed organic matter. Primarily found in places that have low rates of decomposition, such as bogs and swamps.

Perlite – A naturally occurring mineral formed by long-term hydration of volcanic glass.

Petiole – The stemlike attachment, or stalk, between a stem and the leaf.

Pinnate leaf – A leaf that is subdivided into leaflets or pinnae. Leaves can have multiple levels of such division.

Raceme – An inflorescence characterized by having flowers arranged on the main stalk, attached on short stalks, and equidistant from each other along the main stem.

Rhizome – A horizontal, underground stem often used for plant vegetative reproduction.

Sagittate – Arrowhead shaped.

Sori – Reproductive structures found on ferns.

Spadix – A type of inflorescence characterized by many closely-packed tiny flowers on a stem, usually surrounded by a spathe.

Spathe – A leaflike bract that at least partially encloses the inflorescence of a plant.

Succulent – Any plant with modified, thickened leaves or stems for the purpose of storing water.

Syconium – The type of inflorescence specific to figs, comprised of a hollow, fleshy receptacle, within which are multiple ovaries.

Tepal – A floral structure that is either a petal or a sepal (not clearly differentiated). Tepals are often observed in lily flowers where the outermost whorl of the flower is made of sepals that appear petallike.

Transpire/Transpiration – The process of water uptake into a plant and subsequent release through stomata as a vapor.

Tuber – A plant's underground, vegetative reproductive structure. Or a starch storage organ.

Umbel – A type of inflorescence characterized by many short-stalked flowers that emerge from a common point, similar to the ribs of an umbrella.

Variegated – The appearance of irregular markings of a second color, usually white, but it can be any color.

Vermiculite – A glossy, flaky, silica-based mineral, commonly used as an additive to soilless growth media.

Whorl – The arrangement of plant parts (usually floral structures) that radiate from a central point.

AUTHOR BIOS

DR. KIT CARLSON earned her PhD in plant microbiology and pathology at the University of Missouri, and conducted her postdoctoral research at Virginia Tech, focused on molecular diagnostics of plant disease. Kit has been a botany professor for nearly two decades. During her tenure, she has served thousands of students and developed and instructed more than 15 different plant science courses. She and her students have conducted and published research on a wide range of topics, including plant disease, medicinal plants, ethnobotany, public land, science education, and more. She is also the author of *The Book of Killer Plants* and coauthor of *Foraging: A Guide to Edible Wild Plants* and *The Book of Invasive Species*.

AARON CARLSON is an award-winning naturalist recognized for his contributions to observing rare plant species in their native habitats. Aaron received his BS in biology and wildlife at the University of Wisconsin–Stevens Point, and attended the University of Missouri for his graduate work in limnology. When not working as an educator or lab technician, Aaron spends his free time observing and documenting the life histories of lichens, plants, fungi, and animals. Aaron lives in southern Wisconsin with his wife, their two children, and their poodle. He is also the coauthor of *Foraging: A Guide to Edible Wild Plants* and *The Book of Invasive Species*.

ABOUT CIDER MILL PRESS BOOK PUBLISHERS

Good ideas ripen with time. From seed to harvest,
Cider Mill Press brings fine reading, information, and
entertainment together between the covers of its creatively
crafted books. Our Cider Mill bears fruit twice a year,
publishing a new crop of titles each spring and fall.

"Where Good Books Are Ready for Press"
501 Nelson Place
Nashville, Tennessee 37214

cidermillpress.com